Praise for *The Most Important Game*

We have had the great pleasure of having Paul explore his game with us at our VISION 54 golf schools in Phoenix, AZ. He has always impressed us with his curiosity, open-mindedness, competence, determination, and work ethic.

Now, Paul has put together his best mental game reflections to inspire all of us and invite us to explore for ourselves. Anyone who loves the game of golf will enjoy these essays and find lots of ways to utilize their lessons on and off the course.

> Pia Nilsson and Lynn Marriott, award winning LPGA and PGA coaches, bestselling authors of *Be a Player* and *Every Shot Must Have A Purpose*.

I love *The Most Important Game*! It's full of wonderful advice. I have had the pleasure of working with Paul on my own game and have been applying many of these principles throughout this year. I have discovered a renewed sense of joy in a game I have played for forty-nine years.

> LeeAnn Fairlie, Three-time Oklahoma state women's amateur champion. Four-time state women's Mid-Am champion. Member, Oklahoma Golf Hall of Fame.

Golf is one of those unique sports that asks us to dig deep into our inner self if we are in any way to master its complexities. Exploring this space with Paul as your guide in *The Most Important Game* will help you to navigate golf's challenging waters and elevate your performance.

> Dr. Andy Walshe. Founder and Chief Performance Officer, Liminal Collective.

Paul has a unique ability to connect the dots and help us learn from the most surprising people and experiences. His reflections help us navigate through golf's mental game dynamics, and - more importantly - the challenges that are part of everyday living. He shares his wisdom in the same way he shows up for everything - genuine, authentic and with a smile.

> Jay Hennessey, Vice President, Baseball Learning and Development, Cleveland Guardians.

Emerging from every story and reflection are Paul Monahan's energetic presence, years of coaching experience, and keen observations about the game we love. A must read for the golf course and beyond.

> Bruce D Schneider, PhD, Founder, iPEC Coaching and author of *Energy Leadership*.

I don't golf, and yet I cannot put this book down. Not because I intend to golf—I don't! But, because the insights are immediately transferable to my work. Want to learn to loosen your grip and tap into curiosity and your sense of play to grow? This book transcends golf. Full stop. Read this book.

> Dr. Kathleen Boyle Dalen, Consultant, Speaker, Coach. Founder and Principal of KBD Consulting.

"If you ain't having fun doing it, you ain't doing it right." That was my father's motto in life, and he loved playing golf up until a couple of months before he died at 92. That could also be the title of Paul Monahan's book.

The mental game isn't just about technique—it's about attitude, relaxing, and making golf a source of joy in our lives. *The Most Important Game* is full of great hints to increase enjoyment, yield better shots, and decrease the stress and frustration that leads to bad shots and worse golf.

> CAPT Bob Schoultz, USN, Retired.

As a lifelong struggling golfer, I wasn't sure that I was the best person for Paul to solicit feedback from. After reading the book, I can say without reservation that the wisdom that Paul has included here is on point and extremely relatable whether you are a passionate golfer, a parent, or just someone trying to get it right every day. Thank you, Paul, for this gem.

> Rob Nielsen, CEO, All American Leadership.

There is no shortage of frustration on a golf course or in life. Paul offers insights into focusing more on what matters and less on what doesn't.

> Peter Rea, Ph.D. Co-author of *Exception to the Rule* and *Better Humans. Better Performance*.

Contents

A Personal Note From Tim Graves — 1
A Personal Note From Todd Graves — 7
Acknowledgments — 11
Dedication — 13
Introduction — 15

Chapter 1
Stoicism and the Single Plane Swing — 21

Chapter 2
Playfulness — 25

Chapter 3
Expectations — 29

Chapter 4
Responsibility Mindset — 33

Chapter 5
Emotional Awareness and Success — 37

Chapter 6
Jack Was on to Something. — 41

Chapter 7
Fear and Starbucks — 45

Chapter 8
The Sun Will Come Out… — 49

Chapter 9
Managing My Potential — 53

Chapter 10
  Small Adjustments   57
Chapter 11
  Who Are You Being?   63
Chapter 12
  Carpe Diem   69
Chapter 13
  Elongate Your Focus   73
Chapter 14
  Recharging the Batteries   77
Chapter 15
  Playing Not to Lose   81
Chapter 16
  Choke No More   87
Chapter 17
  Possibility Thinking   91
Chapter 18
  Where Are You Looking?   95
Chapter 19
  LUV and Golf   99
Chapter 20
  Social Connection and Golf   103
Chapter 21
  Lessons from a Triathlete   109
Chapter 22
  Get in the Arena   113
Chapter 23
  Bill Murray is Serious   121
Chapter 24
  Perspective   125
Chapter 25
  Opportunities are Everywhere   129

Chapter 26
- **Mastery Orientation** — 133

Chapter 27
- **Miss It Fast** — 139

Chapter 28
- **Stay Curious, My Friends** — 143

Chapter 29
- **Think Give, Not Get** — 147

Chapter 30
- **A Little Inspiration** — 151

Chapter 31
- **A Great Lesson** — 155

Chapter 32
- **Practice Slower & Play Faster** — 159

Chapter 33
- **My Lesson in Acceptance** — 163

Chapter 34
- **It's Not Magic, or Is It?** — 169

Chapter 35
- **Critical Moments** — 175

Chapter 36
- **It's the Journey** — 179

A Personal Note From Tim Graves

Paul has been a positive influence at Graves Golf Academy since the day he joined us as a single-plane-swing student at a three-day instructional school in July 2015.

It wasn't long before we began to understand what Paul was all about. Soon, we invited him to work with some of our staff and then eventually with me and the rest of our team at Graves Golf.

To give you a sense of the kind of person and professional that Paul is, I want to share a story that illustrates his compassion for others and his interest in helping people grow.

A few years ago, Paul began joining us as a mental game expert during our 5-Day Alumni Camps at our academy in Lake Nona, Florida. During these schools, we spend time in the classroom, on the course, and in practice areas performing exercises and drills to help our students cultivate better skills and build a more positive mental game. Paul's role was to help our students think more productively about the game.

During one such school, Paul and I were facilitating together on the first morning of the week. He took the group out to the practice putting green for a mental game exploration, and it unfolded as follows:

1. Paul gave every student a sheet of eight labels. Four of the labels had positive words printed on them (i.e., Happy, Positive, Encouraging, Loving, etc.). Four labels had negative words on them (i.e., Sad, Negative, Discouraging, Unhelpful, etc.).
2. Paul told the students to stick one of the positive labels on another student and repeat that four times until all the positive labels were gone from their sheet. They peeled each of the four labels off the page and picked a student to put it on (I participated and found this very easy: pick another person and put a positive label on them).
3. Paul then told the students to stick the negative labels on their fellow students until the four negative labels were gone. (I participated in this and found it *very hard* to do.)

After the exercise was completed, Paul discussed with the group the distinctions between positive vs. negative self-talk, how it's easy to talk positively about another, and how it's hard to label another negatively. But also how easy it is to talk negatively to yourself and how difficult it is for so many to talk positively to themselves. Ultimately, Paul encouraged us to think about how positive self-talk can greatly enhance one's chances for improvement on and off the course.

On the second day of our school, we always start with a question-and-answer session about the previous day's teaching. I typically ask the students how they think the day went and if anyone has something they want to talk about.

Immediately, one of our students raised his hand and said, "I thought the mental game exercise we did on the green yesterday was a complete waste of time, and in my opinion, all we did was litter." (The labels had fallen off some of the students' shirts and blew around in the breeze.)

I have to be honest—and many of you who know me can probably predict my response—I was not very happy with this student's negative comment. I was very close to escorting him out of the school.

I can only assume Paul saw my initial reaction. Before I responded to this student, Paul stopped me in my tracks, stood up, and asked if he could address the question.

Paul asked the student why he felt that way. Then, he engaged with him about why he thought the exercise was a waste of time and engaged the student in a discussion about the student's mental approach to golf.

Come to find out, the student's frustration wasn't about the exercise at all. It was about the discouragement he felt every time he practiced because he expected better results faster. It was also about how he was expecting his golf game to help reduce the pressure he was feeling at work.

Paul invited this student to explore what he thought the intended lessons from the exercise were and how those lessons could be used to change his perspective in all areas of his life. Paul used his coaching skills to carefully and compassionately bring out the real challenge for the student.

I was completely taken aback. Paul turned a negative situation (and one that I was probably going to make more negative) into one of the best Q&A sessions I've ever heard or been part of. I went from being so mad I was seeing red to having a tear in my eye listening to Paul's encouraging conversation with this student.

At the end of the morning discussion, the students got up and left the room to start our next exercise. After the last student left the room, I turned to Paul and said, "That might be the greatest and most encouraging thing I have ever heard anyone say to one of our students."

Paul replied, "Remember, Tim, when the student is ready, the master will appear."

At first, I thought he was talking about the student. Then I realized he was talking about me and anyone else in the class that morning who was open and ready to hear that message.

I will never forget that morning and how Paul

handled that situation. I grew a little bit that day, and our students grow every time they are around Paul.

As you read this collection of essays, I hope you will enjoy Paul's reflections on this amazing game.

Tim Graves, PGA
Co-Founder, Graves Golf Academy

A Personal Note From Todd Graves

In the tapestry of life, some individuals illuminate our paths, guiding us toward our potential with unwavering dedication. Paul Monahan is one such luminary, a beacon of wisdom and compassion whose mission has touched the lives of leaders, athletes, and performers across the spectrum. As a friend and witness to Paul's remarkable journey, it is an honor to introduce *The Most Important Game*. This book is not merely a collection of stories about the game of golf; it is a testament to Paul's mission to help us go deeper and explore what it means to be at our best.

During the time I have had the privilege of knowing and working with Paul, I have witnessed his transformative impact on countless lives, including my own. His mission is unequivocal: to help individuals realize their true potential, to kindle the fire of growth within them, and to inspire them to embark on a journey that goes beyond the surface and delves into the very core of their existence.

The Most Important Game beautifully encapsulates Paul's philosophy born from years of dedication to personal development, spiritual growth, and holistic transformation. This is not just another golf book—it's an exploration of the interplay between the inner world of the mind and the external manifestations of our lives.

Paul understands that the seeds of meaningful change are planted within us and nourished by self-awareness and a willingness to embrace our shortcomings. Through his heartfelt anecdotes, profound insights, and gentle guidance, he encourages us to approach our inner landscapes with a sense of wonder, to dance with our shadows, and to find delight in the unfolding mystery of this amazing game—if not life itself.

The pages of this book are imbued with Paul's distinctive ability to bring joy to the process of self-discovery. The journey of finding oneself can be daunting, even intimidating, but Paul's unique approach transforms it into an exhilarating adventure. He recognizes that the pursuit of growth should be accompanied by a celebration of life itself—a celebration of our quirks and uncertainties, as well as our aspirations.

If you've had the chance to spend time around him, you know that Paul's accepting style is the cornerstone of his teachings. He creates an environment of trust and openness that allows individuals to be vulnerable without fear or judgment. This approach is rooted in his authenticity and his deep understanding of the human experience.

In a world that often urges us to wear masks, Paul's welcoming embrace invites us to remove them and stand unguarded, ready to explore the uncharted territories of our hearts and minds.

An example of the transformative power of Paul's coaching lies in his work with the Graves Golf Team. His involvement in nurturing the spiritual growth of our team speaks volumes about the potency of his work. He has been instrumental in guiding us toward a new paradigm—one in which the pursuit of excellence is intertwined with a soulful connection with our work. Our team members have not only grown as individuals but fostered a culture that serves our customers on a level that transcends mere transactions to one that creates meaningful, lasting relationships.

In *The Most Important Game*, Paul reveals the wisdom he gained along his journey and his genuine commitment to serving others. With every turn of the page, readers will find themselves not only enjoying stories and insights but also embarking on a transformative voyage—one that invites them to question, reflect, and explore their potential.

As I reflect upon Paul's friendship and mentorship in my life, I am reminded of the quote by Rumi: *"The wound is the place where light enters you."* Paul has a remarkable gift for helping us embrace our wounds, understanding that they are gateways to growth, and through them, the light of our true selves shines forth.

In a world that encourages us to hide our wounds, *The Most Important Game* reminds us that true healing and growth emerge from our willingness to embrace our vulnerabilities. Paul's reflections call for us to be open to recognizing that through those cracks, the light of transformation finds its way in.

The Most Important Game is a manifestation of Paul's legacy of empowerment, joy, and transformation. It's an invitation to step into any arena with renewed vigor, armed with the tools to unlock your true potential anytime you practice or play. As you read it, let this work also be an invitation to embark on your journey of self-discovery, one that embraces the shadows as much as the light and leads you toward a profound connection with your potential.

With gratitude for the wisdom shared within these pages,

Todd Graves.
Co-Founder, Graves Golf Academy

Acknowledgments

Long before I began my private coaching practice, I was fascinated by the mental game elements of high performance. One of my mentors is Bruce D Schneider, a highly accomplished psychology professional, coach, and a terrific athlete with a passion for golf. Bruce and his team of coaches inspired me to take the leap into executive leadership coaching in 2011, and I have never looked back. Thank you, Bruce.

In 2014, Bruce and two of his colleagues developed a tool to help golfers, athletes, and other performers understand the energetic dynamics that were responsible for peak performances. I completed a certification in Bruce's COR.E Performance Dynamics™ model and started using its concepts and tools with my clients.

The following year, I discovered Todd and Tim Graves, who were teaching the Moe Norman Single Plane Swing to thousands of students every year at their Graves Golf Academy instruction schools. I thought that Graves Golf Academy would be a perfect platform for me to test Bruce's COR.E Performance Dynamics™ principles, plus maybe I could learn to play the game of golf at a whole new level.

I signed up and attended a three-day GGA school at Prairie Landing Golf Club in West Chicago. I was totally hooked.

Soon after that, Todd and Tim invited me into their Graves Golf Academy world—first as a coaching resource for one of their young instructors, then for their team, and eventually, their customers. (Likely, many of you are reading this book.)

In 2018, I began spending time instructing at select specialized GGA instruction schools, where Tim and Todd gave me a platform to teach serious players about what it takes to optimize their mental game on and off the course. I owe Tim and Todd—two brilliant, extremely hard-working guys who have built an incredible company—a debt of gratitude for trusting me to help them and their constituents.

The opportunity they gave me at their live schools and on their website to publish the articles and reflections in this book helped me to formulate and solidify my thinking on the mental facets of the game we love and enjoy so much.

The chance to explore the dynamics of high performance in a golf context has made me a better golfer, a better performance coach in every domain that I practice in—plus a better husband, father, and colleague.

Dedication

To Paula, Brian, Joe, and Kevin—all the inspiration I ever needed.

Introduction

When I was a young golfer, I was a complete maniac on the course.

I was immature, had zero perspective, and led with a hot Irish temper that my mom said I was born with. That temper nearly always showed up when I played, mostly in the form of throwing or smashing a club (or three). I couldn't handle losing golf balls, missing easy putts, and being so terrible at a game I thought I should be able to play well.

I grew up playing ice hockey in the winter and baseball in the summer. I was a pretty good athlete with decent hand-eye coordination. So, about every 17th shot on the course was somewhat pure. I imagined in those pure-shot moments that I had finally figured out the game.

But you already know that's not how golf works.

When I was twenty-one, I was playing a late afternoon round at the St. Bonaventure University course in Olean, NY. I had shown up as a single and was paired with a couple of guys my age. On the very first hole, I hit a series of terrible shots, completely melted down, and threw one of my clubs into a nearby tree while I let a few expletives fly out of my mouth.

The guys I was playing with were incredulous. One of them said, "Hey, buddy—you gotta calm down. That's insane."

I had been acting like that on golf courses for ten years, and nobody had ever challenged my idiotic behavior. My brothers thought I was a lunatic whenever I acted up on the course, but they never said what that guy did that day. His comment surprised me.

Fast-forward six or seven years. I was playing a regular Saturday morning round at Sunset Golf Course in Fort Erie, Ontario, with a couple of my brothers and some friends. On the 11th hole, I chunked an easy wedge shot into the lake near the green.

Cue the emotional explosion, right? Not this time.

I calmly went to my bag, dropped another ball, and set up to hit the shot I originally intended to play. But then I plopped that one in the lake, too. Then I did it again. And again.

For those scoring at home, I was I lying 9 at that point, having dumped four balls in the water. But the younger insane Paul, who would have normally emerged after the first shot into the lake, did *not* show up that day. (Sorry to disappoint you.) The older, more mature Paul casually took out another ball, put it down, took a deep breath, and *finally* executed the shot he had envisioned.

Once the ball landed on the green, my playing partner turned to me and said: "That was amazing."

Surprised, I asked, "What was amazing?"

"Dude—there was no emotion at all. You just kept trying to hit the shot. And you never freaked out. I would have dumped my whole bag in the lake three shots ago!"

That's when I realized something had changed in me. Yes, I was playing the same game I had played when I was twenty-one, but it seemed that I had begun to master another game.

Zig Ziglar used to point to his head and say to his audiences of business leaders and sales professionals, "Your business is never good or bad out there. It's only ever good or bad up here."

What if that were also true about golf?

I believe that playing great golf is not just a function of how you manage your outside game. It's also a function of how you manage your inside game so that you can be at your best when it means the most.

Most golfers approach the game as an outside-game-only endeavor.

I understand why. If what we see on TV each weekend is any indication, it seems that success in golf is primarily a function of tuning up your *outside game skills*—your swing mechanics that allow you to hit the ball far, pure, and straight and to make every putt.

The truth is that learning to hit the ball well is

important. In fact, it's a must-have skill when it comes to scoring. So, I don't blame you for spending a lot of time on the outside game. You should.

But there's a catch.

You see, focusing only on the outside game is fine until it isn't. It's fine until:

- It's time to tee off on number one in front of a large group of players.
- You need to hit that long approach shot over the water.
- You just hit your drive OB for the third time today.
- Your buddy just went one-up with two to play.
- You have a seven-footer on 18 to break 80.

Suddenly, you're no longer thinking or playing like that smart, confident, skilled player who was crushing it just ten minutes earlier.

There's another game in golf that nearly everyone is aware of, though practically nobody spends time developing. It's the *inside* game, the one you play between the ears. It's what I call *The Most Important Game*™. Mastering it makes it possible to show up on the course and perform at your best, no matter what is happening.

The Most Important Game is a collection of essays about the mental game of golf written over the past seven years, primarily for the Graves Golf Academy community of golfers. (You're about to read the words: single plane swing a lot, a reference to the swing model taught by Todd and Tim Graves for more than two decades.) My hope is that it can help you think in fresh ways about the game and inspire you to try out a few new ideas that might improve your play.

Each chapter is presented as closely as possible to how it was originally published (with some light editing) and includes a short introduction to help understand the sentiment I was trying to express.

The book is set up so that each chapter stands by itself as a separate concept. You don't have to read the chapters in order, nor read more than one in a sitting.

While it is by no means a requirement, you may decide to integrate key insights from these chapters into your own game. Here's how that could look: start reading *The Most Important Game* by picking just one chapter that seems appealing to you.

Then, put the book down and see if you can apply the big idea from the chapter to your pre-game routine, your practice, your on-course play, your putting, etc. Challenge yourself to make the concept come alive for you and become part of how you approach the game.

Then, pick the book up again and read another reflection, starting the process all over again.

Before you know it, you will have sharpened your inside game skills. You will have strengthened your mental game. And you just may be surprised at what happens to your enjoyment of the game and even your scores.

May you be blessed with good fortune on the course and off.

Fairways and Greens!

-Paul

Chapter 1
Stoicism and the Single Plane Swing

It is hard to overstate the hero status that James Stockdale achieved with the POWs he served with in captivity. Looking back on this article, I understand now that I may have served the reader by also emphasizing this: Sometimes, things in life are hard, and it is important to say so. In fact, by saying so, we are better prepared to overcome them. That's among the most important lessons Stockdale and his men learned. Although I would not compare learning to play golf with surviving a prisoner of war camp during the Vietnam War, they both offer lessons for all of us on approaching difficult things. Golf is a hard game, and we ought to say so.

James Stockdale was one of the greatest military heroes the United States ever produced.

As a Navy pilot and commander, he flew over 200 combat missions during three deployments in Vietnam. He became one of the most decorated Navy pilots ever.

His most significant achievement was after September 9, 1965, when he was taken prisoner after being shot down over North Vietnam.

As the highest-ranking Naval officer to serve as a prisoner during the war, Commander Stockdale's leadership among the POW population was legendary. He was credited with saving the lives of hundreds of American POWs over his eight years of captivity.

(If you want to be inspired by someone's capacity to positively influence others, read Stockdale's essay, "Courage Under Fire.")

Years after the war ended, Stockdale was asked how he coped with the challenges of being a prisoner under such horrific conditions. (Stockdale and others, including the young aviator, John McCain, were routinely beaten and tortured.)

He explained that he never lost faith that things would turn out okay. He believed he would prevail and be a better person for having persevered through the struggle.

But here is the interesting part. When asked about his impressions of those who did not make it out of the prisons—the soldiers, sailors, and airmen who perhaps lost the will to go on—Stockdale said the optimists struggled the most:

> Oh, they were the ones who said, "We're going to be out by Christmas." And Christmas would come, and Christmas would go. Then they'd say, "We're going to be out by

Easter." And Easter would come, and Easter would go. And then Thanksgiving, and then it would be Christmas again. And they died of a broken heart.

Good to Great author James Collins described Stockdale's observation as the *Stockdale Paradox*. Stockdale said, "This is a fundamental lesson. You must never confuse faith that you will prevail in the end—which you can never afford to lose—with the discipline to confront the most brutal facts of your current reality, whatever they might be."

It turns out Commander Stockdale had studied Stoicism, the ancient Greek philosophy, in graduate school. Among the critical tenets of Stoicism is that happiness comes from accepting each moment as it is. I love how Stockdale's perspective and Stoicism generally relate to the human development process and the Single Plane Swing.

Neither the challenges we face nor what's at stake when we learn to play golf at a higher level are as grim or high as those American POWs faced—they're not even close.

But the human psychological dynamics are similar. We can learn a lot from Stockdale's experiences and apply much of what we learn to the Single Plane Swing and playing golf at a higher level.

The Single Plane Swing journey—in fact, any endeavor of change or transformation—requires faith and discipline. It requires faith that you will prevail and the discipline to forge ahead even when experiencing challenges and setbacks.

What do faith and discipline look like for those learning the Single Plane Swing?

Trusting in the process allows you to replicate the Moe Norman swing model that Todd and Tim Graves teach. You must believe that if you study it, work at it, get feedback, and repeat the process enough times, your swing will improve, and you will get the results you are looking for.

You don't need to put a timeline on your development or be an optimist. Do the work, and trust that you will make progress.

So, let go of your story about when you will "arrive." Know that you will get there one day. Consider that "arriving" may not be the point in the end.

When you feel like you have plateaued or regressed, discipline yourself in the practice of accepting setbacks and challenges when they happen. As Stockdale might have said, confront the most brutal facts of your current reality and stay in the game. Don't quit.

You know how to do these things. You've done them all your life and experienced a ton of success.

Now, apply these beliefs and practices to your golf game.

Have faith. Be disciplined. Stay in the game. You will prevail.

Chapter 2

Playfulness

I love this article for a couple reasons. First, it is a story reminding us to reconnect with the joy and playfulness we brought to our experiences when we were kids. Second, two terrific characters are involved. Tom Lagos was a fellow Ohioan who attended many GGA schools over the years and was a joy to golf with. Sadly, he passed away a year or so after this article was published. Gary Gustafson—another perennial GGA 5-Day school guy—has a great attitude and an incredible work ethic.

Recently, I heard a celebrity speaking about golfing with his buddies. He mentioned one person in his circle of golf friends whom he particularly admired because of the playfulness the person brought to the course.

The celebrity said his buddies wished they could be more playful, especially on the golf course. He said that the guy he admired almost always played well, seemingly without a lot of effort.

Playfulness is one of those things that eludes most adults.

If you think about it, it's not anyone's fault; it's a product of the society and culture in which we grew up, which rewards serious, adult-like, responsible behavior.

But studies show that the more we can tap into our childlike playfulness, the better we perform—particularly when it comes to skills-based, physical endeavors.

Last spring, Tim Graves invited me to teach at a *5-Day Build Your Game Alumni Camp* in Orlando. If you ever get a chance to visit a 5-day camp, do it. The camps offer a fantastic experience. Teaching at one of the camps allowed me to teach performance mindset concepts to the attendees and work on my Single Plane Swing.

Among the many fantastic learning dynamics Todd and Tim create in the 5-day camps are live scenarios designed to replicate competitive situations and related pressure we may encounter in our weekly games at home.

One of the scenarios is a bracketed putting contest called "21" that lasts from Wednesday to Friday. The winner earns lots of cool swag and bragging rights for a whole year.

I played in the contest that week, facing the eventual winner in the semi-final round, the virtual putting buzzsaw, Gary Gustafson.

After an incredible hour-long quarterfinal match against Tom Lagos, an excellent competitor, Gary crushed me, 25–2 in about fifteen minutes!

After our match, I asked him about the secret to such a fantastic performance. Gary shared that, while watching the game between Tom and me, he noticed a five-year-old boy putting on the other end of the practice green. The boy was with his mom, goofing around on the putting green. We had seen him, too. He was a pretty cute kid and a tremendous little putter!

Gary noticed two things about the boy's putting. First, he was putting remarkably well for his age, and second, he was putting rather quickly.

Gary equated the boy's speed with playfulness. In other words, the boy didn't overthink each putt. Gary noticed the boy's joy and ease each time he stepped up to the ball, took a look at the hole, and pulled the trigger.

So, Gary approached his upcoming match in a spirit of playfulness akin to the little boy's. He stepped into his putts carefully and deliberately, trusted his line, and pulled the trigger, resisting the urge to overthink the setup.

Man, did his strategy work. His putting was amazing!

Throughout our (very short) match, Gary made a bunch of long putts and plenty of shorter ones. When he wasn't making putts, he came super close, so he picked up points. His strategy was impressive. I had a pretty good seat for that show.

I think Gary's approach is a good lesson for all

of us, regardless of the level of competition or the situation. The strategy is good whether playing golf, in critical leadership moments or negotiating a sale.

We nearly always perform better when we trust our ability to do the thing and step into it without much overthinking. Todd Graves calls it "playing empty."

While multiple dynamics determine success in a skills-based performance such as golf, a spirit of fun and playfulness goes a long way to enhance one's performance.

So, try this the next round you play or the next time you practice. Be intentional about not overthinking. Adopt a playful mindset and step into your shots.

Play the game. Have fun. Don't overthink it.

There's a reason we call it *playing* golf, right?

Chapter 3
Expectations

I remember watching John Rahm explode onto the PGA Tour in 2016 with immediate success and several high finishes. He was exciting to watch. He was often compared to that other fiery Spaniard, Seve Ballesteros. However, on more than a few occasions, it seemed Rahm's expectations got the best of him. Over time, we have seen Rahm mature on the course, but I often wonder about those early successes and how they shaped his expectations about what playing golf on the PGA Tour should look like. In this article, I encouraged readers to set their expectations aside and loosen their grip on outcomes.

It is fascinating how much potential there is for our expectations to negatively impact our experience and our ability to perform at our best.

While watching the last round of the Waste Management Phoenix Open, I heard one of the CBS announcers—I think it was Peter Kostis—comment on John Rahm's challenging day.

After three solid rounds, Rahm began his final day in second place. Following a phenomenal 2017 season in which he earned his first victory and ten top-ten finishes, he was in a position to win another event.

But after sixteen holes, Rahm was at 2 over par and needed to be 3 or 4 under par to be in contention to win. His frustration was pretty evident.

Kostis commented that Rahm's biggest challenge in 2018 would be managing his expectations.

What did he mean? He meant Rahm had to be careful not to set his expectations too high for his 2018 performances.

We perform best when we drop our expectations, metaphorically speaking, leaving them in the car. This lets us see our reality—the game, the shots, the putts, etc.—more objectively and helps us avoid the risk of allowing our stories to cloud our perspective.

Not long ago, I attended the *Graves Golf Academy 3-Day School* in Orlando, the inaugural instruction school of 2018.

On the first day of the school, Tim Graves and his staff emphasized starting the Single Plane Swing process with the shortest golf move possible—the putt—by leading a putting lesson.

As I interacted with students during the putting lesson, I noticed how many struggled with their mental game. Yet, we were simply practicing putting.

Tim suggested we practice matching the putting stroke model and advised us not to worry about sinking putts. He reminded us that, rather than worrying about sinking putts, we should make sure we were hitting "checkpoints." If we get good at executing the checkpoints, we will make putts.

Here's what I saw happening. Guys became frustrated when they weren't sinking putts—some guys were *extremely frustrated.*

These were brilliant, accomplished people. They knew how to listen and follow directions. But, they were stuck in their expectations.

When we get stuck in our expectations and view reality through the lens of hope, we can only be satisfied if those expectations are met. Makes sense, right?

But what happens if our expectations are not met? You guessed it—disappointment, or worse, frustration.

That day, the guys on the putting green were missing putts they expected to make. So, they experienced those misses with disappointment and frustration. They forgot about the purpose of practice.

What would have happened if they'd set their expectations aside?

They likely would have performed better throughout the exercise. They also might have:

- remembered the purpose of the practice session
- not worried about the result

- focused on the process
- worked on matching the putting model
- enjoyed the experience
- learned
- and maybe even been a little more fun to be around.

I often tell my clients that the tighter their grip on their stories or expectations about what should happen, the harder it is to experience their reality productively, especially when things don't go as they would prefer.

If you want to get better at golf or anything else, you must drop your attachment to results and focus on the strategies for producing them, such as gripping the club correctly, starting with a proper address, and matching the swing model.

When you miss a putt or hit a ball poorly, remember that such events are neutral. They are neither good nor bad; they just are. Learn to see what happens in your environment as a neutral incident rather than a catastrophe if it does not meet your expectations. Learn to see outcomes that do not align with your expectations as opportunities to learn and master new skills, no matter the context.

Like John Rahm or the participants in our GGA schools, we all would benefit by loosening our grip on our expectations or dropping them altogether.

Chapter 4
Responsibility Mindset

Elite performers in any field are (typically) great at self-reflection. They learn to focus inward to assess their situations fairly and objectively. Additionally, they can quickly put into context outcomes related to specific experiences. This story about Olympic gold-medalist Ted Ligety is a perfect example of how we always have a choice about how to carry ourselves with respect to the outcomes we experience on the golf course.

Ted Ligety was among the favorites to win gold in the Giant Slalom in 2018 at the Olympics in Pyeongchang. Having won gold in 2006 in Turin and again at the Sochi Games in 2014, along with world championship titles in 2011, 2013, and 2015, Ligety is known as the King of the Giant Slalom.

Unfortunately, in 2018, there would be no gold medal for Ligety in Pyeongchang. After a slow first run, Ligety finished the event, tied for fifteenth place, far out of the medal standings, and a long way from a gold medal. Even more disappointing, he didn't perform well enough in his second run to move up in the standings.

I don't think anyone would begrudge Ligety if he were to look for something or someone to blame. "I didn't have the right equipment." "The conditions were poor." "The food in Pyeongchang was terrible." "My coach didn't prepare me well."

But Ted Ligety didn't say any of those things. In fact, I doubt he even thought of them. Instead, he stepped up and took ownership of his results: "That first run was purely me not having the right approach and going hard enough and going straight and clean enough. That's all on me. Nothing to blame but myself for that first run."

Then he added, "The second run was a mini step in the right direction, but not anywhere close to the giant leap I needed to do anything. I tried to step it up a little bit more but didn't have the speed in the legs today. So, that's how it goes sometimes."

I love that. Here's why. Ted Ligety knew who was responsible for his results on the hill—he was. He did not pretend that others (or other things) were to blame to save face or lessen the pain of his loss.

Instead, he stayed true to himself and was honest about his reality.

The highest achievers among athletes, leaders, and other performers don't blame others when things go wrong. They seem to know intuitively that their achievement depends, first and foremost, on their actions.

How can this mindset help your golf game?

I believe any successful endeavor must include a responsibility mindset, which means never blaming others or things when something goes wrong. A responsibility mindset is rooted in the belief that we control our destinies and that our thought processes, decisions, and actions drive our successes and achievements.

We all know someone who blames everyone or everything else for what happens to them.

Such people often say things like: "He was talking in my backswing. That's why I hit it out of bounds." "She didn't pack my rain jacket, so I lost the match." "I missed the putt because these greens are terrible."

While such people might believe what they claim about what caused their disappointing outcomes, the objective reality is much different.

If I were their coach, I would challenge their notion of cause and effect and help them understand what happened. I would point out things like:

"You hit it out of bounds because you did not deliver the clubhead squarely to the ball."

"You lost the match because your opponent scored more points than you."

"You missed the putt because you misread the break."

Why is it important to know this?

The sooner you see your reality objectively, the easier it will be to develop the skills you need to perform better. (Like squaring the clubhead to the ball more regularly, scoring more points in your matches, and reading brakes on the greens more effectively.)

I encourage my clients to learn to distinguish between what is true for them and the objective reality.

Once they learn to see the truth or objective reality, their mental and emotional dynamics improve, and they can work more productively toward their goals: more fairways hit, more greens in regulation, fewer putts per round, etc.

Operating from blame is a trap that limits our potential at any moment.

Operating from objectivity without the weight of judgment—or the stories the create judgment—is liberating.

Free yourself. Be responsible. Stop blaming. Period.

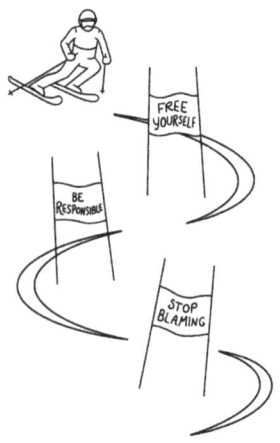

Chapter 5
Emotional Awareness and Success

Years ago, I heard Jerry Seinfeld and Michael Richards reminiscing about The Seinfeld Show. At one point, Richards, amazed that Jerry had noticed a particular detail, said, "See? You don't miss a beat. You pick it all up." Jerry replied, "Well, it's in the air. It's in the colors." I love that because it reminds me that the concepts and lessons that lead to breakthroughs or personal development are all around us. They are in the air and in the color of our experiences. They are available to anyone who takes a moment to notice them. Here is another example of that.

You must develop skills to lead, parent, or play golf better. But you also must get better at "tuning in" to the mental and emotional dynamics that support or limit your ability to perform at your best.

Expanding emotional awareness is the primary work I do with my clients. I help them understand how the events around them impact their thought patterns and, ultimately, their actions or performance. When they get better at seeing how events on the outside impact their "internal mechanics," they can build the emotional resilience necessary to perform well, no matter the situation.

So, how do you develop higher awareness? I believe that happens by focusing on a couple of simple concepts.

First, you must learn to notice what you think about in challenging situations and the feelings and emotions those thoughts produce.

This means learning to pay attention to how your brain interprets each moment. For example, you can notice your thoughts about a driver who cuts you off in traffic and the feelings and emotions your thoughts generate.

If you are like most people, your initial thought might be, "What's the matter with that jerk?" The feelings that accompany the thought may be anger or frustration.

Simple right?

Next, you must notice how your thoughts impact your behavior. This is key because the quality of your interactions and your performance depends on what you do.

To notice how thoughts affect behavior, you must identify how your thoughts influence your actions. What do you do when the guy cuts you off in traffic? Do you step on the gas and ride his bumper for the next mile? (That would show him!) Do you raise what my wife calls "the swear finger?" (Hey! You're number one!) Or do you ease up on the gas and make a little room for him?

Often, the behavior is a reaction to emotions and the thoughts that preceded them. You can get a lot of clues about how productive your thinking is by analyzing your behavior when you experience strong emotions.

Recently, one of my clients told me a story about how he quickly tuned in to his thoughts and emotions.

He was traveling through a busy airport and experienced a long TSA line. When he finally arrived at the x-ray belt, a TSA agent instructed him to go a different route. My client admitted he pretty much wanted to strangle the guy. However, once he realized that the behavior directed by his feelings or thought pattern might not serve him well (strangling a TSA agent is probably frowned upon), he began to reframe the situation.

His awareness enabled him to anchor to a richer story; he focused on how the TSA agent was doing his job. He reminded himself there was nothing personal about the agent's directive, however inconvenient and annoying. This allowed him to respond more productively. His ability to summon awareness of the reality of the circumstances allowed him to achieve his objective (to get home) with less stress because he chose to engage politely with the agent.

So, my client was successful for two reasons. First, he noticed or paid attention to his thought patterns. Second, he recognized when the thoughts and related emotions threatened to influence the moment negatively and redirected his thoughts, yielding a more effective response or behavior.

Life is an inside game—all of it, always, including relationships, work, leadership, parenting, traveling, and the Single Plane Swing journey as well. Learn the physical skills for sure. In addition, whether you want to improve your golf or life, remember that working on your inside game can make a big difference in your experiences on and off the course.

Chapter 6
Jack Was on to Something.

It's hard to imagine a golf conversation about the all-time best players without mentioning Jack Nicklaus. His dominance of the game during his career may never be matched. In 2019, I found a quote from an interview with Jack that revealed something about his on-course mindset that I had never heard before. Nicklaus developed his commitment to staying even-keeled as a young golfer after observing what happened when he played poorly. His observations and commitment to staying levelheaded changed his relationship with pressure. Nicklaus was on to something (duh!). In the reflection below, I wanted to encourage the reader to consider how adopting a strategy like Nicklaus's might help them develop their own strategies for staying calm and feeling inner peace while playing.

Jack Nicklaus was on to something when he discovered a truth about himself as a young golfer and used his discovery throughout his career.

Nicklaus was known as a powerful golfer. He was a big, strong, thick, and burly guy who could pummel the ball unlike anyone else when he arrived on the PGA Tour in the early 1960s.

Many considered Nicklaus's mental discipline among the most important aspects of his game. Hale Irwin recently remarked, "[Jack] had a capacity to stay in the game all the time. He didn't ever beat himself."

Ultimately, a combination of superb shot-making skills and a highly developed mental game on the course allowed Nicklaus to amass his incredible record in tournament play. His achievements include eighteen amateur wins, eighteen major wins, runner-up in nineteen majors, top five in fifty-six majors, seventy-three PGA Tour wins, and 117 wins overall. It's an unbelievable resume.

In a documentary, Nicklaus offered insight into his successful mental game when he said, "I learned when I was a young kid that if I got excited, I *couldn't* play."

Nicklaus learned how to calm himself by tapping into an inner calm and peace to stay in the game without becoming either too excited, upset, or frustrated. As Moe Norman might have phrased it, he taught himself to take an alert attitude of indifference into his play. This allowed him to play well in clutch moments.

(The one-iron on 17 at Pebble Beach in the 1972 US Open. The 40-foot putt on 16 at the 1975 Masters. The tee shot to three feet on the 16th at

Augusta in 1986. The putt on 17 at Augusta in 1986. Or Jack's favorite example of clutch play under pressure: the par, par, par finish to win his first Open Championship in 1966 at Scotland's Muirfield Golf Links.)

At the 1963 Masters, it poured rain during the Saturday round, and the tournament was almost canceled. But Nicklaus decided not to let the weather bother him, shooting one of the day's best rounds and winning his first of five green jackets. Nicklaus had learned to reframe his experiences in order to operate at a high level no matter what was happening. After he retired, he said, "Pressure affected me in a positive way."

Clearly, Nicklaus's shot-making abilities were incredible. (Great skills are nonnegotiable, so keep working on the model.) His commitment to staying calm was also a huge part of his success.

His mental game success formula was so simple. So accessible to everyone. Not that hard. It takes some awareness, intentionality, and commitment to see your world more productively and objectively interpret the events in your environment.

You may not be able to bomb it down the fairway like Jack Nicklaus did. (Or today's equivalents—Brooks Koepka, Justin Thomas, Bubba Watson, Xander Schauffele, etc.) But you *can* achieve the same level of calmness and mental skill Nicklaus did with practice and attention in the following ways:

- Tuning in to your own confidence level at any moment.
- Recognizing that your feelings—fear, anxiousness, nervousness—are products of your thinking.
- Anchoring to more objective views of reality not overly laden with judgment.
- Remembering, as Todd Graves likes to say, "Stuff happens. The rest is just a story."

Keep this in mind as you work on your game this winter. The most important opportunity in your game right now might not involve picking up your clubs but rather learning to cultivate a productive level of calm and inner peace that you can take to the course.

Chapter 7
Fear and Starbucks

Let's face it: for most golfers, the struggle on the course can be traced to what I call the "small f" fears. These fears show up in many domains of life. Learning to acknowledge and move productively past them is an incredibly worthwhile investment of one's time.

My wife Paula and I took in a comedy show a couple weeks ago in Cleveland with our sons Joe and Kevin. We saw Nate Bargatze, a brilliant comic from Nashville, TN.

Successful comics learn to tune into their fears. They understand that fears are universal and know that these fears can be the basis for great comedy.

Toward the end of Bargatze's set, he told a great story about a recent experience at his local Starbucks. The story was about a funny communication mix-up. However, it was rooted in his fear that the customers and employees of Starbucks would judge him as unworthy of being a Starbucks customer.

You see, Bargatze—a self-proclaimed introvert and quiet guy—confessed that he had always been intimidated by Starbucks. That's what made his bit so funny. I remember being intimidated by Starbucks, too.

The first time I entered a Starbucks years ago, I wanted coffee, but it was so intimidating! The smart customers and baristas spoke a language I had never heard. Would they look down on me? Would they judge me if I ordered a "small" instead of a "tall" coffee? What the heck is a venti anyway?

There were so many options. What is a caramel macchiato? Did I ask? Heck no. I ordered something simple and got out of there before they found out how little I knew.

Over time, I figured out the Starbucks lingo. I developed the courage to ask about the differences between a latte and a cappuccino. I overcame my fear of the Starbucks experience.

Bargatze's comedy was so good because it hit home for many audience members. I laughed so hard because he tapped into my experience of overcoming an irrational fear.

Fear comes in many forms. When we are learning something new, it often shows itself in our need for credibility.

The need for credibility is a primary need we all have. It's rooted in the hope that the people around us will:

- value our contribution

- appreciate our skills and intellect
- not judge us harshly.

The fear driving Nate Bargatze's experience at Starbucks can easily come up for anyone trying to learn a new skill, especially the Single Plane Swing.

You show up to the range and begin to work through the positions. But once it is time to actually hit the ball, you revert back to old habits because you know that at least then you can hit the ball and not look like a complete idiot!

At that point, your fears and your need for credibility drive your behavior. At that moment, it is more important to swing the club incorrectly as long as the ball flies in the air in a way that others won't judge and deem you an idiot golfer.

But holding on to that thinking will never allow you to progress.

As you work on mastering your Single Plane Swing this year, resolve to tune into your fears and eliminate them.

Become aware of your fears by asking yourself things like:

- How true is it that others will think less of me if I miss-hit a few shots on the range?
- How true is it that others care about how well I hit the ball?
- What is the real reason for spending time at the driving range?

Stop caring so much about what others may think about you. Instead, enlist others to help you see what you cannot. The fearless Single Plane Swing golfer seeks out the GGA instructor and asks: "How did that look?" or "Did that swing match the model?"

When you visit us at a GGA instruction school this year, forget about trying to impress; focus on learning. Ask our instructors: "What did you see?" And then listen to and accept their answer.

Living a life of ease and freedom on the golf course or in everyday experiences is worth striving for. It starts with identifying your true fears and working to move past them.

Chapter 8
The Sun Will Come Out...

The journey to mastery is never a straight line. It seems there are always times of growth, plateau, and even regression. I remember feeling like I was on an extended plateau on my Single Plane Swing journey. The weight of it all inspired me to write the reflection below after visiting our son in Nashville. As I revisited this, I remembered two things. First, the ideas and insights we need are all around us. We only need to pay attention. Second, struggling is often what we experience when we are growing.

It's always darkest before the sunrise.

Have you ever heard that before? I have. I'm not sure if it's true.

Regardless, the metaphor works for me. It goes something like this:

Occasionally, it seems like we will never emerge from our struggles. While plodding away in the darkness (a metaphor for struggle), things can begin to feel heavy. This can cause us to lose hope about transcending the darkness and overcoming the struggle.

But then something magic happens. After working a long time on something, breakthroughs happen. Insights appear. Hope grows. The struggle ends.

Then the sun comes out, and life is good again.

My wife and I recently spent the weekend in Nashville with our son Kevin, a young musician and producer.

For people like Kevin and his peers in the music biz—smart, talented people working very hard on their passions but who have not yet achieved the level of success they are aiming for—the darkness of struggle can be an impediment to realizing dreams.

Kevin and his music-industry friends are inspiring to me because they are so committed to the work that they never stop moving forward. They are sometimes tempted to compare themselves to others. However, those who thrive in these conditions are dedicated to the process of improvement. They don't get stuck (very often or for long) where they happen to be at any point. They trust so much in the process that success is already theirs, even when it seems dark.

This is as it should be. The struggle is necessary to grow talent.

A decade ago, the author of *The Talent Code*, Dan Coyle (also a friend of the Moe Norman Single Plane Swing Community), revealed the importance of embracing struggle when learning new skills. Coyle references advances in science that show how struggle builds and reinforces the network of neurons in our brain, allowing us to successfully develop the skills we need to perform at high levels.

The Talent Code reveals the importance of struggling while practicing.

As you prepare for another year of golf, you may be facing struggles as you work to match the Single Plane Swing and become a better golfer.

Since we never know how long the process will take—there are many factors and variables to consider—the struggle may feel like it will never end. If you feel that way, it's okay.

You are exactly where you should be.

That said, there are a few things you can do:

- Stop comparing yourself to other golfers. Compare yourself today to the golfer you were yesterday. This is the only comparison that matters.
- Reframe the Single Plane Swing journey. Remember that it is not about if you can get it; it's about when. Reframe your journey. Make it less about *if* you'll be successful—you will be. Loosen your grip on *when* you have to be successful. Accept that success has its own timeline.
- Step outside yourself when things get really heavy and focus on serving others for a little while. When we operate from the perspec-

tive of "service to others," our mindset is much more positive and productive.
- Enjoy the journey and small victories.
- Know that success is already yours. Growth comes from struggle.

The struggle is necessary for growth. Struggle layers your neurotransmitters with the amazing brain protein sheath (myelin) that will make changes to your swing long-term. Struggling in practice ensures you can take your swing onto the course and play better.

So, if it feels a little "dark" right now, it is okay. The darkness is part of the process.

With continued focus, intentionality, practice, and maybe a little reframing, the sun will come out for you and your swing. I have no doubt.

Chapter 9
Managing My Potential

The Don Byers story ("oldest collegiate golfer ever") from 2018 is fun to read and contemplate when the game seems easy and the hole seems as wide as a bucket. But there is also a great lesson about how powerful the fear of failure can be and how tapping into playfulness and joy can unleash the best in us.

Staying connected to one's true potential at any moment comes partly from high consciousness. High consciousness occurs when you have an awareness of who you are and a good sense of what your life is all about.

Primarily, I think of high consciousness as the mental state whose hallmark is the ability to contextualize or put things into proper perspective easily and quickly.

Don Byers understands what it's like to stay connected to his potential at any moment. In April 2018, Byers made history as the oldest person ever to play a college sport when he teed up his golf ball as a member of the Bellevue University Men's

Golf Team.

As the story goes, Byers, a sixty-one-year-old father and grandfather, happened to play a round of golf in August of 2017 at his home course (Champions Run) with Bellevue's head golf coach Ron Brown. Byers had worked on his game for the previous few years and had worked his handicap down to scratch. He played very well the day he golfed with Brown.

Brown was impressed and joked to Byers about whether he had any eligibility left. It turned out the former baseball player had four years of eligibility left due to an injury he sustained before his freshman season at the University of Nebraska, Omaha.

So Beyers, who owns his own insurance agency, was recruited by Brown and later joined the Bellevue Bruins golf team.

It wasn't easy for him. As he tells the story in a Golf Channel feature story, Byers was nervous about making the team and wanted desperately to earn a spot in the top five on the team so he would qualify to tee it up in tournament play.

Byers reported that: "I didn't want to fail. I wanted to play well right out of the chute and impress everybody. You start pressing when it doesn't happen that way, and it slowly falls apart on you."

But to combat those nerves, he said: "I found myself having that care-free attitude again. Just go out there and have fun." Eventually, he earned an opportunity to play in the Bruins' last tournament of the season as a 61-year-old freshman. He made history as the oldest collegiate athlete ever.

How did he earn that spot? In part, I believe he was able to put his experiences into proper context and anchor them to the thought patterns he knew could produce a better experience for him. Ultimately, I think he tapped into the playful and joyful feelings that are so much a part of his golfing.

Don has developed the skill of managing his current potential.

What does that mean? It means he has learned how to stay in productive thought patterns while playing golf and play his best golf no matter the stakes or the situation.

As a leadership and performance coach, I often help my clients cultivate an idea called Managing My Potential.

I encourage them to look inward and tune in to the thought patterns that connect them to their potential in the moment, as well as the ones that block their access to that potential.

Managing My Potential happens for me when I am aware of the mental and emotional dynamics that keep me connected to my true potential at any given moment.

Managing My Potential is about expanding self-awareness. It's about creating high consciousness (awareness) about the present moment as it unfolds so I can cultivate proper context and perspective. It allows me to see things objectively and without a lot of judgment.

As the snow falls regularly and the cold sets in a little deeper in many places, the opportunities to play are fewer for a little while. But you can always work on your mental game skills by tuning into your mental and emotional dynamics.

When that happens, you will make the most of every round. You will tap into joy and passion and play with ease. You will access the best in you on that day. And you will play better golf!

Cheers!

Chapter 10
Small Adjustments

The message highlighted in the reflection below was unexpected. And so was the messenger—the rental car bus driver in Oklahoma City, OK. His message was terrific: reaching your goals happens by committing to moving forward and making small adjustments every day, one after another. I remember thinking how right he was and how it meant that I didn't have to make giant leaps today... that small gains day after day would take me where I wanted to go. The small adjustments metaphor is perfect for learning to play just about any game. My new friend Marty said the formula is pretty simple: commit to being better, make small adjustments every day, and eventually accomplish whatever you want. Not always easy. But simple.

Sometimes inspiration comes when you least expect it.

I recently had a chance to spend a couple of great days at the Graves Golf Academy HQ in Edmond, OK. It was a great visit full of great interactions, creative ideas, stepping outside my comfort zone, learning from the great team at GGA, and even time for a little golf with Tim.

Something happened at the end of my trip that made it especially inspirational.

I ended my second day with Tim, Todd, Chandler, Shannon, Blade, and others and headed to the airport late in the afternoon. I had stayed as long as possible at Rose Creek Golf Club, and I barely had enough time to make my flight.

The first order of business was to drop my rental car off at the Will Rogers World Airport and hop onto the shuttle that would deliver me to the main terminal.

As I approached the shuttle bus, a guy greeted me cheerfully and offered to put my golf clubs onto the bus. I noticed his name tag, so I said: "Thanks, Marty."

He replied with a big smile and lots of energy. "Thanks for calling me Marty."

Marty was the shuttle bus driver. When all the passengers had boarded the bus, Marty took his seat behind the wheel, and we headed to the airport. He picked up the microphone and began making what sounded like a pretty routine courtesy announcement:

> Good afternoon, ladies and gentlemen. My name is Marty, and I will be taking you on the four-minute ride to the main terminal here at Will Rogers World Airport. I hope you

enjoyed your stay in the Oklahoma City area.

I was only sort of listening. But then it got interesting. Marty continued:

> And if I may, I would like you to consider this.

Uh-oh, I thought. Where is this guy going with this?

> You will be on an airplane headed to your destination in a few minutes. As the pilot points the plane down the runway and throttles up the engines, he will make many small adjustments to the engine, wings, and other control surfaces so that you will soon be soaring high in the sky.

There was more:

> I invite you to consider that life is like that as well. If you commit to making small adjustments every day in your own life, you, too, can set yourself up to soar. To achieve all you want to. To be who you want to be. And to create the life you want.

Whoa! Who is this guy?

Marty was articulate, polite, happy, and positive. His message was simple, thoughtful, and expertly delivered. And he inspired me to pause and think. That's not what I expected from the driver of that shuttle bus.

It struck me that much of what I talk about with my performance clients can be thought of in the way Marty described.

Small adjustments made often over time lead to profound changes.

That's the same message we've heard from Todd, Tim, and others regarding skill development in the Single Plane Swing arena: Start slow. Feel position one. Then, feel position two. Learn what proper rotation onto your trail leg feels like. Ask for feedback on one thing. Then another, and so on.

Small adjustments made often over time lead to profound changes.

That's the same message I offer regarding building a more productive mental game. Learn to be a little more aware of your thoughts today. Then, become a little more aware tomorrow. Learn the language of performance energy. Then, learn how performance energy shows up for you on the course. Notice how it impacts your ability to hit the shots you desire or prevents you from playing your best.

Small adjustments made often over time lead to profound changes.

We all get impatient sometimes, and it's easy to fall into the trap of needing a big change immediately.

But immediate big changes are not always possible or even advisable.

Part of Marty's message was this: take the pressure off yourself to fix what you want this week in your swing mechanics or mental game skills. Instead, get on a path to mastery.

Commit to making small changes over a long period. Trust that you will create the change you want. That's how you improve your swing mechanics. And that's how you raise your consciousness and performance energy (read mental game) on the course.

So, the next time you happen to be at the Oklahoma City Airport rental car facility, look for Marty driving your shuttle bus, and listen carefully to his advice!

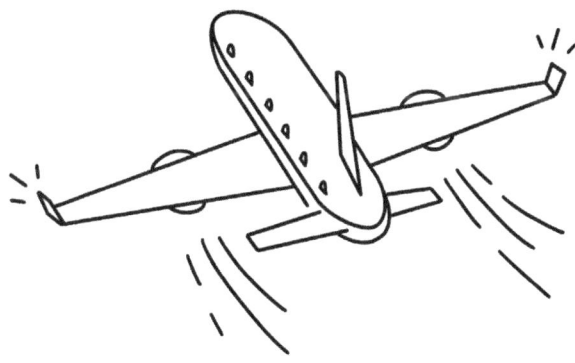

Chapter 11
Who Are You Being?

One of my favorite coaches likes to talk about identity. He has observed that most people form their identities over time, and they "become" those identities. They believe they "are" those identities. The problem is that our identities are not as permanent as we think. We can shape who we show up as in almost every moment. Said differently, we can take on the identity of almost anyone we want, whenever we want to. We are not stuck with who we think we are—for better or worse. But most people don't think in these terms. Instead, they limit their potential by locking themselves into identity and personality. This reflection followed a fun experience I had that illustrates this point perfectly. By tuning up your awareness of who you are being, you can make important shifts when it serves you.

In early May, I had the pleasure of attending the 5-Day Alumni Camp in Orlando and spending time with some great Single Plane Swing students, including Bill and Debbie Miller.

The Millers have been attending GGA schools for a while, so you may have run into them. (I hope so because they are awesome to be around!) They are no strangers to performing at a high level since they spent many years at the highest levels of the sport fishing world on the Gulf Coast of Florida.

On Thursday of Alumni Camp week, we had an on-course experience, a sort of *Big Break Orlando* at the Eagle Creek course. The GGA team likes to call this event *"Clay's Revenge"* because veteran GGA instructor Clay Farnsworth sets up the challenges on each hole.

It's a fun event for the attendees, a chance to hit real shots on a great golf course, take what they have been working on all week, and see what it looks like in a simulated game setting.

That day, my role was to help the players get out of their heads and inspire them to stop thinking so much and start playing the game. Even though it feels like it sometimes, hitting a golf ball is not a cognitive endeavor; it's an athletic one.

A couple holes into the Big Break event, I caught up with Bill. His game was off a little—and he wasn't hitting the ball very cleanly (to be charitable). And he knew it, but he couldn't get his technical thinking and swing mechanics out of his head.

As a result, he was in a bit of a struggle.

The good news is that the previous day, Bill and the rest of the group heard Todd Graves talking about the concept of the Alter Ego—the notion that we can take on any identity we want to, such as Jordan Spieth, at any time to solve a performance challenge. So, pretend you are Jordan Spieth if you want to putt better or Moe Norman if you want to hit long straight drives. You get the idea.

There is some pretty compelling research that shows the performance value of this approach.

(In fact, here is a great place to start—one of our favorite resources on the concept: *The Alter Ego* by Todd Herman.)

Before the Big Break round that morning, I challenged the group to ask themselves: "Who am I being?" and "Who does this moment call for?" Both are designed to inspire players to think about an identity they could take on to help them perform better on the course.

So, when I caught up with Bill, and he was struggling, all I had to ask was, "Who does this moment call for?" Immediately, Bill's eyes lit up. He was thinking about someone. There was someone he could call upon—an identity—as a great model for high performance on the course. In fact, it was his former self.

It turns out that Bill, at one point, was a low single-digit handicap golfer. Over time, his professional fishing, his family, and other pursuits got in the way of playing as much golf, so it had been a little while since he connected with that version of himself. But the important thing was that he could *conceive of an identity* that happened once to be his. It didn't matter that he channeled his former self during the Big Break event to help him get out of his thinking and back into an athletic game-playing mode.

With a big smile and fresh perspective, Bill stepped back into the game he once knew with an identity that could help him perform better than he had been playing that day. He had a plan.

A couple of holes later, I watched Bill completely turn around his on-course experience. He was playing the game, not overthinking, being creative, hitting great shots, and having fun.

Later, as we reflected on the turn of events, I told Bill how much fun it was to watch him take on that new identity.

Bill replied, "You came up, and I asked you what was going on with my swing. I wanted to know what the quick fix was… what I could do to play better. You gave me the 'channel your 6-handicap former self' pep talk. And then you said, 'You're an athlete; play like one.' I tried to visualize that and stopped thinking mechanically, and just played. I got much better, and we used my shots a number of times, including a clutch drive on 18."

So, as you get ready to give yourself a little pep talk ahead of your next round, remember that you have a choice about the identity you assume when you show up on the course. Will it be that weekend golfer who just can't buy a break? Or the one who always hits it into the woods off the #7 tee? Or the one who never pars #12? Or the one who will never master this "flexed lead knee" thing?

Or will you take on a more powerful identity as a player with a pro-level attitude who understands and appreciates the variability inherent in the game, accepts every bounce, and is ready for his next shot to be his best shot, no matter what?

I think I know the answer.

Hit 'em straight!

Chapter 12
Carpe Diem

Sometimes, an old idea seen in a new light is enough to inspire us to greater achievement. The notion of "Plucking the day" rather than "seizing it" may represent a fresh way for you to think about your game. It may offer a way to be more present and in the moment while you play. Learning to play golf is hard, and making progress is even harder. You must act with intention. It also helps if you remember to savor the moments on your journey as well.

If you are of a certain age, you may remember the scene from the classic 1989 movie *Dead Poets Society* where Robin Williams implores his young students to "Seize the day, boys. Make your lives extraordinary."

In that scene, Williams, as Professor Keating, leans on the Latin phrase carpe diem, loosely translated as seize the day, from a poem written by the Roman poet Horace in 23 BC.

The context of Horace's poem and carpe diem reminds us that we are not guaranteed tomorrow;

life is fleetingly short, and it has two implications. First, if you are not intentional about creating exactly what you want in your life, before you know it, you will run out of time. Second, life is meant to be enjoyed. If you forget to enjoy today, you will waste a precious gift.

In the past thirty years or so, carpe diem has become a popular way of reminding people to take on today, seize it, crush it, make it the best day ever, "win" the day, or dominate the day.

That's all well and good. However, carpe diem is more accurately translated as "pluck the day." In other words, approach today as if it were a piece of ripe fruit on the tree of life, ready to be plucked and enjoyed.

Why is this subtle shift in meaning important? If today is to be plucked, there is no need to chase it down, grapple with it, fight it, seize it, or overcome it. It is here, ready to enjoy. You need only to step up and pluck it. The phrase implies that you live in a state of abundance. The tree of life is essentially right beside you and full of ripe fruit.

A masterpiece day need not be rare; you can make such days happen if you're prepared to be intentional.

As you begin the new year and think about all you want to accomplish in golf in 2022, consider what shifts in thinking and actions would be required for you to pluck the day. Then, ponder what that would mean for how you approach your Single Plane journey.

Maybe it would mean getting after the things that are important to your development journey in golf, like waking up a little earlier tomorrow to stretch and prepare your body for practice. Perhaps you might eat a little more sensibly this week, so you have the stamina to play your best for a full eighteen holes. Or maybe you'd send that video to the GGA coaching staff so they can help you transition from the top.

It might also involve enjoying and appreciating more moments, big and small, such as the smell of the grass on the course you are playing, the sound of a perfectly hit shot, the feel of a well-struck putt, or the satisfaction of keeping your head down on that slippery eight-footer on the eighteenth.

You might also take the focus off yourself and your own needs and turn your focus toward others to inspire, influence, serve, or make a difference in the lives of those around you.

Maybe you will do one thing each day this year to get you closer to your goals, make you 1 percent better, or improve the life of another.

The day is yours for the taking. Get after it, yes, and savor it too. No need to seize it or wrestle it to the floor. Just pluck it. Step up and do things that get you closer to what you want to create in the game you love and the life you lead.

Here's to an extraordinary new year. Carpe Diem!

Chapter 13
Elongate Your Focus

Phil Mickelson's win at the 2021 PGA Championship was one of the most epic performances in golf history. In the weeks following Mickelson's win, stories began to emerge about his preparation leading into the championship. It seems that Phil spent a fair amount of time working on his mental game, and in particular on "elongating his focus." Mickelson's intentionality about building his mental game skills paid off that weekend. He played at his best when it meant the most. The same approach can pay off for anyone willing to dedicate the time and attention to it.

As Kevin Streelman lined up a twenty-foot putt on the tenth hole in the final round of the 2021 PGA Championship at Kiawah Island's Ocean course, CBS announcer Trevor Immelman commented on how Streelman and his playing partner Louis Oosthuizen were playing. Neither had been able to put together a meaningful move up the leaderboard toward Mickelson and Koepka. Both had posted rather lackluster scores on the front nine.

Oosthuizen shot even par, and Streelman was two over.

Immelman said, "This feels like a must-make for Streelman. These guys are leaking energy." Streelman missed that putt and went on to shoot a 3 over par 75.

Attempting to realize our full potential at any moment, no matter the stakes or the situation, is worthwhile. The challenge is that performing at our best can sometimes feel elusive.

Why? What gets in the way?

Immelman's language intrigued me and reminded me of a conversation I'd had a few weeks earlier with Shawn Huls, the Director of High Performance for the Cleveland Browns. Yes, the same Cleveland Browns who improved from 6–10 in 2019 to 11–5 in 2020.

Huls, an expert in human performance, has worked in the NFL for many years and before that with the Navy SEALs' Elite Team 6. He likes to use two metaphors to describe what gets in the way of great performances—leakage and seepage.

According to Huls, leakage happens when your positive and productive thinking "leaks" out of your head and is replaced by negative thoughts like doubt, worry, anxiety, and fear. Such negative thoughts lead to overthinking and diminished confidence. Leakage shows up when your inner dialogue includes phrases like: "You loser; you hit it over there again," or "You are so stupid; I can't believe you did that," or "You're never going to get this swing down."

Similarly, Huls claims that seepage occurs when negative words from those around you "seep" into your head. Examples may include phrases from your tribe like: "Why do you bother working so hard at that?" or "Why do you stick with that Single Plane Swing?" or "You'll never make putts with a putter like that."

Huls says that if you eliminate leakage and seepage, you set yourself up for more frequent episodes of high performance.

Phil Mickelson was not leaking energy on the Ocean Course on Sunday. In fact, I believe that we will all be talking about his radical mental game approach to the Championship—elongating his focus, staying present, and visualizing and committing to the shot—for a long time. What a remarkable performance for an "old" guy.

Playing well today or any day requires optimizing the skills you show up with that day.

To play well on the course, you must bring intentionality to your processes, just as Phil Mickelson did all day at Kiawah Island.

You must be intentional about not leaking energy or allowing negative energy to seep into your thinking.

Stop the leakage. Practice taming your inner dialogue. Build an internal narrative that you can rely on in challenging situations that *supports* your desire for high achievement on the course. Stop tearing yourself down. Be your biggest supporter instead.

Eliminate the seepage. You do you. Strive to live your best life daily, on and off the course. Stand firm in your convictions and commitment to move boldly toward your goals—fewer putts per round, hitting more fairways and greens, more sand saves, or whatever. Don't let other people's negative paradigms hinder your goals, dreams, or aspirations.

Chapter 14
Recharging the Batteries

I know many people on a journey of golf skill development who are so passionate about the game and their desire to improve that they forget to take breaks. No high-performance human endeavor is successful over the long-term without some version of an ON/OFF execution cadence. Creating intentional down time on your journey can be unbelievably effective. Sometimes, you only need a slight shift in focus.

A few weeks ago, my wife, Paula and I were talking about the importance of recharging our batteries. We talked about the value of stepping back occasionally from the physical and mental demands of things we face to gain a fresh perspective on the endeavors most essential to us.

Last week, LPGA star Lexi Thompson withdrew from the women's British Open, which will be played this week at the venerable Royal Lytham & St. Anne's Golf Club. Citing the events of the past eighteen months on and off the course (including a crushing loss at the ANA Inspiration in 2017, her grandmother's passing, and her mom's cancer diagnosis), Thompson expressed her desire to step away to, in her words, "recharge my mental batteries," for a couple of weeks.

A couple of days ago, a very talented client of mine, an accomplished Single Plane Swing golfer, put his clubs down for the weekend to focus on anything but golf, which had been a significant source of frustration for him the past couple of weeks. Like Thompson, my client also needed a mental break.

We all need such breaks from time to time. Do you take such breaks when you need them?

Bruce Lietzke passed away this week. He was famous for his ability to take the all-important mental break, stepping away from the game to get another perspective. I guarantee that his immersion in collecting and re-building cars served him well on the golf course in ways that might surprise you.

Bruce once told his caddie Al Hansen that he wouldn't touch his clubs from the end of the 1984 tournament season to the beginning of the 1985 season. Hansen, dubious about Bruce's claim, stuffed a banana under his driver-head cover, expecting Bruce to discover it soon. To Hansen's amazement, he and Bruce found the rotting banana months later, right where Hansen had put it.

Sometimes, a mental break comes from a shift in focus.

We plan to emphasize this in the Mental Game

School in Chicago on August 31st.

Instead of struggling with hitting a position or trying to match a swing model, you will learn to shift your focus and thrive mentally on the golf course through insightful learning experiences.

No worries or concerns about the swing model. Just a new focus on *playing* the game.

I hope you consider how important this kind of break could be for you.

Regardless of whether you attend the school, consider the benefit of creating shifts in focus to keep your perspective fresh and productive.

Take a break. Read a book. Go for a walk. Get away. Do what you do differently.

This is how the most successful at their craft develop and maintain high mental function and the achievement that comes from it.

Chapter 15
Playing Not to Lose

In this reflection, I waded into risky territory as an armchair quarterback, amateur psychologist, and part-time TV golf analyst, offering my take on the Jean Van De Velde collapse at Carnoustie in 1999. What I find so fascinating about this story is that it seems to be such a great example of the performance dynamics that emerge from playing not to lose versus playing freely with nothing to lose. I believe that we typically perform at our best when we step into each shot from a possibility perspective, unencumbered by the prospect that we might not realize our desired outcome. As I revisited this article, I wished I had written more about operating from abundance versus scarcity. So, I added a couple thoughts at the end of this entry that did not appear when I originally published this in 2018.

The French have much to celebrate this week as their soccer team, Les Bleus, won their first World Cup Championship in twenty years.

With the golf world turning its attention to the

famed Carnoustie Golf Links in Scotland, I am reminded of a time about nineteen years ago this week when French sports fans experienced the agony of defeat after their own Jean Van De Velde let the Claret Jug slip from his grasp at the 1999 Open at Carnoustie.

Known in sports lore as "Carnage at Carnoustie," Van De Velde's crushing defeat might have been one of the most painful sports moments I've ever watched on TV. (The exception may be Bill Buckner's missed ground ball during the 1986 World Series. Ouch!)

With a three-shot lead and one hole to play, Van De Velde's world seemed to unravel right before our eyes. In a slow-motion crash replayed repeatedly since then, Van De Velde made a triple-bogey on 18 to squeak into a playoff, only to watch Paul Lawrie win in a stunning fashion.

As a mental game coach, I am interested in how such epic failures occur. What happened? Did he succumb to the pressure? Did he meltdown on the eighteenth hole because of mental stress? Did he choke?

What happened to Jean Van De Velde turns out to be a little more complex than I once thought. Thanks to a documentary on The Golf Channel, *Go Down Swinging*, we have more insight into what happened and why.

My big takeaways:
Van De Velde played and putted incredibly well for three straight days.

He was playing freely, virtually unencumbered by negative thinking. This allowed him to play, be creative with his shots, and go for the shots he knew he could make. That's how you should always play golf.

In fact, Van De Velde reported that, while many other participants were hitting irons off most tees, he felt he had been hitting his driver well, so that's the club he went with off the tee. It was a very successful strategy.

Also, nobody made long putts like Van De Velde for the first three days. Forty, fifty, and even sixty-footers. The guy had things dialed in. He was playing great and truly enjoying himself.

He did not have his "A" game on Sunday. Not nearly.

This is super important. We all remember what happened on the eighteenth hole—the "carnage." It would be easy to say that he lost it at the eighteenth. But I think certain things occurred before the last hole that sealed his fate.

Here's what I mean. He struggled to hit clean golf shots from the first few holes on Sunday, and his putting was off. He didn't have his "A" game. Why not?

Did he forget how to hit a golf ball straight or how to putt? No. I suspect his brain was cluttered with the prospect of losing.

Even though he may not have been aware of it, I believe Van De Velde was playing to not lose instead of playing to win.

He had never been close to this position—leading the championship after fifty-four holes. My guess is he was in unchartered territory, and his survival mechanisms kicked in.

A funny thing happens in our brains when we get into these situations. The primitive part of our brain designed to keep us alive gets to work. It looks for any threats to survival and works to keep us safe from those threats. The problem is that it cannot distinguish between losing a three-shot lead at The Open and a mortal threat. It sees them both as a major issue.

Van De Velde's struggle on Sunday was a function of his primitive survival brain getting in his way. All of his capabilities and skills that produced terrific results from Thursday through Saturday were no longer accessible.

Paul Lawrie made an incredible comeback.

One of the most under-reported stories of the 1999 Open was that Paul Lawrie began the day ten shots off the lead. Does anyone even remember that Paul Laurie was the eventual winner? He shot a 67 on a day when the average score was ten shots higher than that. That's right. The average score on Sunday was 77.

What allowed Lawrie to thrive on a day when so many others struggled?

First, Lawrie began the day with nothing to lose. His goal was to shoot a low score in order to punch a ticket to the 2000 Masters at Augusta. So, there was some pressure, but not a lot. Lawrie's objective that day was very different from Van De Velde's.

Second, he was playing a course he was very familiar with. He lived about forty-five minutes from Carnoustie at the time and slept in his own bed every night during the 1999 Open. This combination of confidence and comfort helped him to tap into all his skills and make great shots that day.

There's a lesson for all of us here: When we operate from an abundance mentality rather than a scarcity mentality, the game we love is far easier to play.

This is because an abundance mentality helps to short-circuit the threat response in our brain. And when our threat response is not triggered, we have a better chance of showing up at our best.

So, operating from an abundance mentality means you:

- Recognize that you already have enough. i.e., you don't "need" anything.
- Remember that the game of golf has so much to give you every time you play it.
- Can imagine no limit to how many fantastic shots you might hit in a round.
- Believe that you are richer from the experience of playing—whether you win or not.

You never have to play to lose. That's because it's possible to win in so many ways every time you play this great game.

Chapter 16
Choke No More

Choking is something we have all experienced on the golf course. It's not fun, I know. But there are things we can do to prevent the choke. If you work on the fundamentals mentioned in the reflection below, you can drastically improve your capacity to perform in pressure-packed moments. You may not always stick that approach shot over water on 18 to three feet with everything on the line. Still, you are much more likely to make a decent shot, and more importantly, you probably won't dump it in the lake.

If you want to take on some fascinating summer reading during your vacation at the beach this year, read Sian Beilock's book *Choke: What the Secrets of the Brain Reveal about Getting It Right When You Have To*

It is a very interesting read that offers insights into the human brain's inner workings, especially under pressure. You may learn a thing or two about your own experiences on the golf course.

Those who have worked with me, heard me

teach, or read my blogs have likely heard me talk about the human internal mechanics and the simple structural model I use to describe how our brain responds to stressful situations.

You've probably heard me say, "It's not the event; it's how you think about the event that matters most." To put it another way, it's not the event itself but how you interpret it that matters.

As Todd Graves says, "Stuff happens; the rest is just a story."

In *Choke,* Beilock cites numerous research studies about why we are less likely to perform at our best when confronted with stress and pressure.

Choking under pressure does not have to be a part of your golf experience.

Beilock asserts that poor performance under pressure on the golf course is not because of your specific situation; it's because of how you think about it. So, what does that mean for you? How do you control your thoughts about events as they occur in real time? A few things have to happen.

First, you have to be aware, which means tuning into your mental and emotional state while things are happening in front of you in real-time. This makes it easier to notice when unproductive thinking creeps into your process.

Second, you must mentally prepare for crazy things to happen before they occur.

Have you ever noticed that pulling off a successful bunker shot during your round is difficult if you've never practiced it? You may also notice that responding productively to stress and pressure is very difficult if you haven't already developed that skill.

You must practice what you will say to yourself if you miss a critical putt on the sixteenth green. You must speak out loud the words you would use if you hook your tee shot into the water on #10. And you must rehearse your inner dialogue for that moment when your playing partner blows a chance for the two of you to win a big match.

Walter Hagen used to say he could count on making four bad shots in any round. He just didn't know when. So, Hagen was prepared mentally and emotionally for the unexpected. He had a story to anchor to when things went sideways.

Third, you need to practice writing new stories for yourself, productive stories that you can anchor to in challenging moments.

Most of my work with my clients centers on helping them expand their awareness of the mental and emotional dynamics that prevent them from accessing their full potential at any moment.

Today, you have the potential to play golf at a certain level. Your performance is based primarily on your skill and expertise (How you swing the club, hit the putts, etc.) For example, if you can hit a 250-yard drive and hit the fairway 50 percent of the time, your potential today to hit any given fairway is about 50 percent.

However, realizing your potential on the course depends also on your ability to manage your mental and emotional state, which means learning to respond productively to the inevitable challenges.

The choke, even the mini-choke, is simply a function of poor self-management—the inability to realize one's potential because of how stress and pressure insert themselves into your experience.

But the choke is preventable as long as you tune up your awareness, prepare for stressful moments in advance, expect things to go sideways now and then, and develop a productive story to use as an anchor when you need it.

Enjoy your summer reading!

Chapter 17
Possibility Thinking

What is possible for you in your golf game? Shoot sub-90? Sub-80? Break par? I don't know, and maybe you don't know either. If you attach your idea of what is possible to effort, it is easier to roll up your sleeves and focus on the work necessary to achieve your most important goals. As you coach yourself, focus more on what is possible and less on the struggle to reach your potential.

Mastering a musical instrument requires significant investments. Many people I know would love to play the guitar like Brad Paisley. In reality, the personal costs of mastering guitar playing are too high. Most won't invest the time and effort necessary.

A year ago, a young guitarist I know very well was invited to perform at the Grand Ole Opry, country music's most coveted stage. He said his experience at The Opry was unbelievable, breathtaking, and awe-inspiring. To him, ten years of effort and practice had been worth it.

Making it to the Grand Ole Opry wasn't an easy journey for him. His success was never guaranteed. Sometimes, he wasn't even sure he had what it took to "make it." Other times, he wasn't sure he wanted to do the work necessary to get there.

Despite his doubts, he put his head down and powered through his uncertainty. In part because he was passionate about what he was doing and in part because he believed that hard work would take him where he wanted to go.

My country music version of the old Carnegie Hall joke:

Student: *Can you tell me how to get to the Grand Ole Opry?*

Teacher: *Practice. Practice. Practice.*

Where do you want to go with your golf game?

You may not want to win your state amateur title or club championship. But you may have a vision of success greater than where you are right now. That's terrific. It says to me that you believe in your own capacity for growth. (We call this a growth mindset!)

So, how do you get there? First, you must be intentional about where you want to go and the actions you are willing to take to get there. That's the easy part. Second, you must commit to doing the work. That's the hard part.

Here's the thing: we all have a default future. It will show up in exactly twelve months. It always does. If you hang out on the couch until then, it will still show up. I promise. The question is: will you be a better version of yourself by then? Will you be closer to your goals?

If you want to play better a year from now, show up more capably, perform at a higher level, or get different results on the course, you must gain new skills and knowledge. You must do the work. But sometimes you may question whether the investment required is worth it. And that can get you a little stuck.

For those moments, let me suggest this hack: Stop thinking about the costs and focus on possibility. Think about what you will gain—the fulfillment from the accomplishment or the growth and maturity you experience from the journey—instead of fixating on what you have to give up. (How hard it is, how much work it is, etc.)

In my experience, successful people who are growth-minded are also very possibility-oriented. They frame their challenges in terms of what lies on the other side of their efforts. This allows them to tune up their "want to" (passion and desire), and they inspire themselves to go for it.

Their internal dialogue sounds like this:

- "What would be possible if I finally learned to play the piano this year?"
- "What if I finally wrote that book I have been thinking about for the past ten years?"
- "How much more fun would golf be if I developed a world-class short game this year?"
- "Imagine if I could hit a dozen fairways every

time I played."

As you consider your own Single Plane Swing journey, I encourage you to tune in to any negative thinking you may have around personal costs and see if you can redirect that thinking toward possibility and how your life can be so much better once you realize your visions.

I think you will find that this kind of thinking will inspire a bias for action necessary for big accomplishments.

To possibility!

Chapter 18
Where Are You Looking?

In the Summer of 2020, I had a chance to visit an amazing spot near San Diego, CA, where I can engage in two of my passions essentially on the same plot of land. From an inner-game perspective, my visit there made me think about the trap we often fall into on the golf course when trying to avoid danger.

Last week, I visited the Torrey Pines Golf Course just North of San Diego, CA. It is an amazing slice of golf heaven. But believe it or not, the highlight of my trip there was a visit to the nearby *Torrey Pines Glider Port*. This is where grown adults intentionally walk/jump off a 325-foot-high cliff toward the beach below repeatedly. They can't get enough of it.

If I didn't know better, I'd say it sounds a little crazy.

Not to worry, though. They are actually paragliding—floating on the thermal updrafts and ridge lift (vertical winds) created by the ocean breeze moving inland. These fliers gracefully raise fabric wings above them and fly around in the buoyant currents of air for hours. It's really cool to see up close.

While they are doing this, *where they direct their focus* is important. Among other things, they must be aware of their position in space, proximity to other fliers, the ground, and the cliff below them… *as well as* where they ultimately want to go. To fly safely and to achieve their mission, they must avoid fixating on what is right in front of them, even if those things represent potential danger.

Where they look matters for achieving short-term and longer-term goals. Their success as paraglider pilots depends upon noticing what is happening around them while steering toward where they want to go.

In aviation circles, there is a saying, "Where you look is where you will go." You will eventually fly into the cliff if you keep staring at it. It happens. Sometimes, pilots get mesmerized by the things close to them.

My friend and colleague Rob Nielson, a former US Army helicopter pilot, recently told me:

> I remember the first time a flight instructor told me to drop my scout helicopter into a riverbed at 140 MPH with trees soaring above and around us, with about ten feet of clearance on either side of the rotor disc. He told me exactly what you said: Look where

you want to go, and your hands will fly you there.

What do you look at when you play? It is so easy to get fixated on the danger we perceive. The out-of-bounds on the left. The creek on the right. The trap near the green. The branch you are trying to hit under.

The problem is that we can lose perspective when we fixate on these things. We can lose sight of the longer-term objective. The place we ultimately want to get to, our purpose, and why we play the game.

We perform best when we are aware and conscious of everything around us and clear about our ultimate objectives.

Moe Norman famously described the "trouble" on the courses he played as "decorations." In keeping with his philosophy of playing with an "alert attitude of indifference," Moe simply saw these things for what they were and focused on the goal—the fairway, the green, the hole.

Moe trusted that his hands would fly him there.

A lot is going on when you are playing golf. There are many shiny objects and dangers, like the cliff at Torrey Pines or the trees next to Rob Nielson's helicopter rotors. Yes, being aware of them is prudent, but focusing only on them won't serve you well. Only one thing really matters.

Bring your eyes up. Change your language about what you see. (Do you see a sand trap, or do you see a decoration?) Reconnect with where you really want to go on the course. (Forget about where you don't want to go.) Trust that your hands know what to do.

And then step up and hit it there.

Chapter 19
LUV and Golf

One of the most powerful mindsets you can ever take onto the course with you is the one that is forged out of love. So many amazing things happen when we operate from a perspective of love, appreciation, and gratitude. When Southwest Airlines' founder Herb Kelleher passed in early 2019, it reminded me of the amazing influence of love, so I wrote this reflection.

Herb Kelleher passed away recently, a couple days after New Year's Day.

Kelleher (Herb to all who knew and met him) was the beloved cofounder and former CEO of Southwest Airlines.

If you have ever flown on a Southwest flight, you have experienced an organizational culture shaped by Herb's philosophies and leadership.

He was known as a driven, charismatic, and high-energy leader who—more than anything—cultivated an organization where love and respect (for each other and the customer) were foundational to its operation.

For Southwest employees, love is in their DNA. They are based at Love Field in Dallas, TX. Their stock ticker symbol is LUV. And they relish saying things like: "LUV is in the air" in their marketing and corporate messaging.

And from my perspective, it seems they are committed to walking the talk most of the time.

So, what does this have to do with golf?

Southwest's formula for high performance and success is available to you.

When you travel on Southwest, you may notice that the employees seem to have a lot of fun. They are joyful, creative, and playful, which translates into a great flight experience for most travelers.

Kelleher's LOVE paradigm drives the culture of playfulness and fun. It has created one of the best-performing airlines in the industry.

If you want to perform at your best on the golf course, you will do well to consider that cultivating LOVE on the course can be an amazingly successful strategy.

What does that look like?

- How about being intentional about sending warm and loving intentions (aloud or not) toward the people in your playing group? And yes, even toward your competitors.
- How about treating yourself a little better?
- How about an inner dialogue that is supportive and loving toward yourself and others and not the opposite?

I've written and spoken about this in-depth many times at our schools. The research is clear: Operating from a perspective of LOVE cultivates the confidence, focus, and inner calm that produces our best golf.

More importantly, it can also short-circuit your brain's built-in threat response that causes missed four-footers on the eighteenth hole and other choking moments.

So, as you continue to either play some rounds in the warmth and sunshine of the South or Southwest or prepare to play when the sun comes back out in the North—remember that you have a powerful mindset option from which to operate on the course.

LUV may be in the air. But you can be sure that LOVE and great play are on the course!

Chapter 20
Social Connection and Golf

It's interesting how often an insight into the game of golf emerges for me when I am operating in a completely different domain. (The word insight literally means "fresh thinking") While hiking in the mountains of Wyoming in August of 2019, I had an insight about my golf and the social dynamics inherent in it. It came from a surprising source.

Social connection is an incredibly important influencer for all of us. You may not have thought much about its value in a golf context. However, a recent experience made me consider why social connection is a great topic for the GGA community.

Human beings are wired to connect with each other in important ways. (Dr. Matt Lieberman's TED Talk on the neuroscience of human connection is pretty interesting.) For example, when you sense that your need to connect with others (to be liked, loved, appreciated, etc.) is in jeopardy, your energetic presence can shift in significant ways—

and your play can be impacted.

It boils down to this: your ability to stay present in the game you are playing—and to play and perform at your best—sometimes depends on whether you feel like you are being supported by the people around you.

I spent an amazing week in August in the Wind River Mountains in Central Wyoming with an incredible group of leaders and coaches. We were part of a National Outdoor Leadership School (NOLS)-led expedition designed to explore team and leadership dynamics, overcome physical challenges, and reconnect with nature.

One of the elements of the fascinating trip was the team of pack llamas that accompanied us, carrying our food and some of our gear. It turns out that llamas are highly social pack animals and significantly influenced by their social nature.

There were fourteen of us on the trip, along with seven llamas. We were all in the same camp at night, but during the day, when we hiked, we would break up into smaller groups of four or five people. This meant separating the llamas, too. No big deal, right? Well, not if you're a llama!

Each of the llamas had a distinct personality. "Coyote" was young and rambunctious. "Oregon" was mature and calm. "Roper" wanted to lead, and so on. One of the things we noticed was that their performance on the trail depended on the social dynamics around them.

So, if Roper wasn't leading, he would pout. If

Coyote wasn't with his buddies, he was tough to handle. (That's right; some of them seemed to get along with some but not all the llamas.) And if one of them felt challenged, they would spit or kick.

All of this made me think of how we (human beings) handle our interactions with others when playing golf.

Let's face it. Not everyone approaches the game the same way you do. Some talk more than you. Some drink more, use language you don't, or make noises while hitting the ball.

Additionally, others may not approach the fun competition you enjoy the same way you do. They may bang their club on the ground after an errant shot. They may get super-intense with themselves or others.

If you are not careful, you can let other's behaviors impact your own thought patterns—how you experience the game and, ultimately, how you perform on the course.

When I work with golf clients, I always talk about their energetic presence on the course and the social connection influencers that are a part of that dynamic. I aim to help them become aware of what they need from others on the course. This allows them tune in to potential detractors when they occur and reframe their thinking to maintain a more neutral and objective stance.

This way, no matter how the other person behaves, they can still have an enjoyable experience. They can still stay connected to their true potential and play the game at or even above their skill level (and not below it).

How does this work?

Imagine the playing partner who gets super-angry with every shot. You know this guy. Every shot has to be perfect, or they tell themselves (out loud) what a complete idiot they are. They get intense and angry with themselves and maybe even others around them.

How do you react to that guy today? Do you get a little caught up in their drama? Do you get annoyed by their behavior because you "would never do that?"

If you do, you risk being taken out of your game and lowering your performance capacity. Why? Simply because you're thinking about how another person is behaving.

So, how do you turn that around? How do you prevent being taken out of your game by that guy?

First, tune into your own mental and emotional state. Notice what you feel about the situation— ("His behavior is frustrating me.") Next, notice how those feelings affect your behavior. ("I'm getting tense and missing easy shots.")

Then, see if you can isolate the original thought driving your feelings. ("This guy is a total jerk.")

This is super important because your feelings are a product of your thinking. Isolate your thinking, and you can make important shifts in your mental state.

Finally, reframe that thought. ("This guy is acting like a jerk. But he is doing the best he can right now. Maybe I can be a good friend and support him while he is struggling.")

You might be surprised at what happens next if you can do this. Your emotional intensity will diminish. Your feelings will shift from frustration to care and concern. And you can stay connected to your full potential on the course.

All because you shifted your thinking.

Too bad my llama friends will never quite get this!

Chapter 21
Lessons from a Triathlete

When I first started flying regularly, I used to talk to every passenger I sat beside on an airplane. Now, an airplane seat is my refuge, a place to concentrate for a couple hours. I hardly speak to anyone. However, a few years ago, I was compelled to engage a fellow passenger after I noticed a book she was reading. I'm glad I did because she reminded me of one of life's fundamental truths of achievement.

"How do you prepare for a triathlon?"

I recently asked this question of my new friend Alyssa sitting beside me on a Southwest Airlines flight to Baltimore.

Alyssa had opened her reading material for the flight, a large paperback book called *The Triathlete's Training Bible*. It piqued my interest because I am currently working with a client who is preparing for triathlons himself. I was curious to hear what the magic formula was for creating success in this arena.

So I asked my question, then waited for the big reveal.

Her answer was simple and brilliant, reminding me how we can accomplish anything. She said, "Basically, I set a goal, then I break that goal down into manageable action items. Then I commit to executing those action items."

So, for Alyssa, it meant establishing goals in running, biking, and swimming and taking small steps toward those goals every day, every week, and every month. It meant planning her work and working on her plan.

That was the big reveal?

I found myself smiling. This was a young person who clearly understood the template for accomplishment. And she knew it.

Brilliant. This is the template for accomplishing anything important and creating anything you want in your life.

It works for triathlons, building a business, and even learning to play the game of golf at a higher level.

What a great reminder. And what an important Mental Game lesson for those of you on the Single Plane Swing journey.

Set a goal. Break that goal down into manageable action plans. Execute those plans.

How are you approaching your own SPS journey? Are you expecting to reach your goal of shooting sub-80 rounds regularly by next week? Or are you taking a more measured approach?

Think of the productive mindset you can create for yourself if you just break down your goal into manageable action plans and then simply work those plans.

What would it look like?

What would it feel like knowing you were on the path and would eventually get where you wanted to go? Imagine if it didn't matter when you achieved your goal.

Part of creating a healthy and productive mindset on the golf course is to remove the anxiousness and pressure associated with the outcome. When you break down your goal of breaking 80 into smaller chunks, the work within each is easier. It is less "weighty."

This makes it more likely you will arrive at your goal. Not less likely.

So, you don't have to achieve your goal today or this week. Just be on the path, chipping away at your larger goal by accomplishing the smaller goals along the way.

If it is good enough for a triathlete, it's good enough for us!

Chapter 22
Get in the Arena

I played small ball for the longest time, not putting myself out in really competitive situations. I don't doubt that I played golf that way out of fear. I was afraid that my inadequacies would be revealed. (Even though I may have been telling myself a different story.) Since I committed to stepping into a more serious competitive arena, how I see the game has changed forever…and for the better! Whatever you do, give yourself the gift of stepping into the most challenging golf arena you can find, even if it means you fail spectacularly.

Failure has made me a better golfer today than I was just a month ago. Here is why.

I have truly enjoyed my Single Plane Swing journey over the past seven years as I endeavored to play the game at a higher level. I love this path of exploration and growth inside the game that I am on. I suspect you do, too.

But I noticed this summer that I was not testing myself as I should.

My idea of competition had been the Saturday morning money games, scramble-format charity events, and match-play tournaments at my club. All great experiences, for sure. And those helped me experience what it is like to play through stress and pressure.

This year, however, I decided that I needed to test myself in new ways. So, I signed up for a scratch event at the end of July as part of the Cleveland Metroparks annual championship tournament.

I wanted to see what it would be like to play against a much better tier of golfer in a 36-hole event in which every single shot counted. No handicaps. A low score wins. Period.

What a great experience.

First, my results were mediocre at best in the context of traditional outcome measurements. I shot 87 and 92 and finished fifty-fourth out of 70.

Second, while it is easy to dwell on the failures—I struggled off the tee at times, and my iron play was not very solid, plus I took too many putts—what I learned about myself and the current state of my game far outweighs any temporary setback I might be feeling about the results.

I learned this:

My short game was pretty solid.

Todd Graves tells a story about when he shot a particularly high score in a tournament—a 90 or something. When Tim asked how the heck Todd hit a 90, Todd said, "I putted great!"

If you asked how I shot an 87 on the tournament's first day, I might have said, "I chipped pretty well!"

I stayed relaxed through the hitting area, not nervy or jerky, hit my landing spots often, and judged distances well.

If there is one thing that has made golf so much more fun for me over the past few years, it is the development of my short game. Tim Graves' impact here—and his emphasis on the short game—has been profound for me.

My putting needs to be better.

I noticed that I struggled to dial in pace properly.

The greens were set up very fast for this event, faster than I had ever seen them. But no excuses; this will have to change if I am going to shoot lower scores.

Another thing I noticed was that I was not hitting committed putts. I know this, and you know this: we must commit to the putts we are hitting. No vacillating over the ball. Hit the putt you commit to, Paul!

My trail hand gets "rotational" when I am tired.

This was something that surprised me. By the back nine of the second day, I felt the physical impact of being out there. And it showed up as a duck-hooky, early extension kind of a swing off the tee that led to hitting several shots left or even way left.

While this caused a lot of trouble on the course that weekend, it was a very important revelation for me. I am fully aware of something today that I just wasn't that aware of before. Now, I can put a game plan together to stay non-rotational no matter what.

My game needs work.

It's pretty clear: I must hit more fairways and more greens. It's that simple. The numbers don't lie. And there is nothing better than an event like this to be a giant metaphorical mirror to show you exactly where your game needs work. It sounds elementary—but this was a HUGE ah-ha for me.

I need to manage my physical energy better.

I think I overdid the prep in the days leading up to the tournament.

And I need to manage my mental energy better. Great pre-shot routines and great post-shot thinking (i.e., neutral or celebrate), but too much thinking in the play box (Go Zone). Need to be prepared more to be a better athlete in the Go Zone—and not a thinker. (Does anybody know a good mental game guy?)

The real competitor is the course.

I managed to keep a healthy perspective on who my true competitor was that weekend. It was the course and not the guys who happened to be playing in my group.

Golf is funny. We normally think of our competitors as who we play against. But the real competitor is always the course. I believe that is true, even in a match-play event, even if the other person's play is part of the dynamic.

The way this showed up for me was in my course management. Understanding what my next move would be, independent of what anyone else was doing, and not being intimidated by their longer drives or other productive play.

I can play the game on the same playing field as really good players.

How do I know that? Because I did. And I routinely put together lots of good shots. I also went toe-to-toe on several holes with my playing partners, who were low single-digit handicap guys.

For example, the first hole was the number 2 handicap hole with a landing area only twenty-five yards wide. I was the only one in my group in the fairway. I gave myself permission to celebrate that one!

None of this means I expect to shoot better than a plus 2 player in an event like this. But I believe it is possible to play my best golf in an event like this, even if I didn't exactly do that this time.

One of the guys in my group shot 54-39 on day one. He made such a mess of the first six holes and kept saying, "Hey guys, I'm better than this, really." (Irrelevant, by the way.) Turns out he is a 3-handicap and just had a tough day. He shot 78 on day two.

Say what you will about his play or mine; the key is that we were in the arena. That's what matters. That's what will make us better players.

Teddy Roosevelt famously said. "The credit belongs to the man who is actually in the arena."

And if you've not seen it, the full quote is as follows:

> It is not the critic who counts, not the man who points out how the strong man stumbles or where the doer of deeds could have done them better. *The credit belongs to the man who is actually in the arena*, whose face is marred by dust and sweat and blood; who strives valiantly; who errs, who comes short again and again, because there is no effort without error and shortcoming; but who does actually strive to do the deeds; who knows great enthusiasms, the great devotions; who spends himself in a worthy cause; who at best knows, in the end, the triumph of high achievement, and who at the worst, if he fails, at least fails while daring greatly, so that his place shall never be with those cold and timid souls who neither know victory nor defeat.

Read that again. Slowly. And think about it.

It's easy to do a lot of talking. It's harder to do the doing. But by doing the doing, by daring greatly, you set yourself up not for the admiration of others (which in the grand scheme is nice but not worth that much) but for the growth and mastery that come from the experience. And that is what makes it totally worth it.

What's your next-level arena as you move along your own Single Plane Swing journey? What competitive challenge is next for you to test and expose your current game's strengths and shortcomings?

Whatever that challenge is for you, get in that arena. You may experience victory on some level. You may experience failure. But either way, you will be a better golfer because of it.

Hit 'em straight!

Chapter 23
Bill Murray is Serious

Acceptance and presence are core elements of improvisational comedy. Without either of them, it doesn't work. Bill Murray's approach to his life and work is rooted in both. Turns out that they are also effective mental game concepts in golf.

Bill Murray is one funny guy. How often have you seen him joking around and stirring up mayhem at the Pebble Beach Pro-Am? Year after year, everyone wants to see him show up, partly because of the outlandish outfits but mostly because you never know what that guy will do or say.

Dancing with fans in sand traps, posing for pictures, drinking beer with the gallery, nothing seems to be off limits for this wild, fun-loving guy with a larger-than-life personality.

But Bill Murray has a profoundly serious side that may help you think differently about your golf game if you explore it a little.

The stories of Murray showing up at parties uninvited, hanging out for hours singing and partying, and even staying late to do the dishes are legendary. What is this all about?

Turns out that Bill Murray has thought very deeply about how he wants to show up in his life. He wants to play the game of life from a PRESENCE perspective. He wants to be present and in the moment as much as possible to thoroughly enjoy whatever life has to offer.

With a little reflection, it becomes easy to see that his penchant for being present comes from a life in improvisational comedy (as well as a longtime interest in the teachings of Zen Buddhism). As you may know, the first rule of improv comedy is to *accept what is given to you*. So, if you and Bill Murray are "doing improv," and you ask, "Hey Bill, how does that chocolate cake in your hand taste?" Murray must proceed as if he actually has chocolate cake in his hand.

The cool thing, I imagine, about spending so much time operating from a perspective of acceptance is that nothing throws you off. Why not? There are two reasons. First, you have no expectations about what will happen. Second, you have committed beforehand to managing through, around, or past whatever shows up.

Murray has no expectations about what you will say to him. He is fine playing with whatever you present because he has already committed to doing so. Playing is his thing. It's how he lives his life.

The ancient philosophers defined wisdom as

one of the most important virtues. Within wisdom, they identified curiosity as one of its most important strengths. Why? When we operate with curiosity, we see things for what they are and not worse than they are. And perhaps, most importantly, we don't get stuck in the disappointment of unmet expectations.

Murray's zest for life—his willingness to be present and in the moment and play with whatever he is handed—creates an incredible ability to deal with life's challenges in productive ways.

It turns out that Bill Murray is serious about his fun. He is intentional about acceptance, which helps him experience his life the way he wants to. It also helps him to stay connected to his full potential in any moment.

What would it look like if you showed up in your golf game with a little more acceptance instead of loads of expectations and the disappointment that comes from unmet expectations? What would it look like if you were more curious about your golf game instead of demanding that the game give you something?

I think you would enjoy the game more and perhaps shoot lower scores. What do you think?

Chapter 24
Perspective

Here's another example of how insights show up when I least expect them. My mentor, Bruce D Schneider (a very passionate golfer, by the way), taught me that the capacity to gain perspective and context as we move through the experiences and challenges in our life is one of the most important predictors of success. On or off the course, cultivating perspective is one of the most important skills I know of.

I wasn't expecting it.

I was getting ready to board an evening Southwest Airlines flight to Baltimore from my home in Cleveland, preoccupied with thoughts about the latest round of winter weather bearing down on the Mid-Atlantic.

With a two-hour-plus drive to my final destination after landing, would I have to contend with rain, snow, sleet, or even worse, highways clogged with cumbersome, slow-moving traffic? I was hoping that this would not be the case. And I was a little on edge about it, even wishing that the gate crew would pick up the pace so that we get off the ground as soon as possible.

I had scored the A1 boarding position for this flight, so I was looking forward to a prime seat near the front of the plane, ensuring I could quickly exit when we arrived at BWI. I had my plan in place...all we needed was some solid execution. (C'mon, people. Let's get this going!)

Then we started boarding the plane, and everything changed.

It turns out that our flight was an Honor Flight originating in Phoenix, with Baltimore as its final destination. The plane was carrying about forty WWII and Korean War veterans and their escorts heading to Washington, DC, to see the monuments built in their honor. Many of them were traveling there for the first time.

These men fought for our freedoms against incredible odds sixty and seventy years ago. They were in their eighties and nineties, and there was even one who had turned 101 that day. The mood was electric. And I was moved.

I got to shake a lot of hands and even talk to a few veterans who were so happy and appreciative of the chance to be on this trip. In fact, I'm not sure I've ever seen as much pure joy and excitement in a group of adults. It felt like such an incredibly unique and humbling experience.

And then, I noticed that I had forgotten about my need to move things along and get to BWI as fast as possible. And all my worries about the weather, the traffic, and getting to my destination faded away.

But what happened?

The experience with the Honor Flight veterans allowed me to shift my perspective and be more conscious of what life is all about.

I believe it is an excellent lesson about showing up for anything, including your golf game.

All your worries about getting off the first tee, hitting fairways, and making crucial putts pale compared to the big things in life. Your families, relationships, and how you influence your employees, companies, and communities.

Those are the things that are important in life.

So, go for it. Learn to play this game better. Strive for better shots and lower scores. But remember what is essential in your life. Endeavor to be more conscious of what life is indeed about.

A little perspective will help you play this game better and enjoy it more.

Chapter 25
Opportunities are Everywhere

Awareness is the foundation for effective self-management. It's what allows us to recognize ourselves and others in the world around us and contextualize the meaning of each moment that we move through. It's also key to dialing in to the thoughts that drive our mental and emotional dynamics and making important shifts in our thinking when we need to.

Just had a great week in Orlando at the GGA 5-Day Alumni Camp.

It was a fun week of learning, instruction, and growth, as well as some great conversation about what it takes to perform at a high level.

My job at the camp last week was to help the attendees expand their awareness of the mental and emotional dynamics that allow them to show up at their best.

Said a little differently, I was there to help them learn how to tune into their energetic presence—the mix of physical, mental, emotional, and other elements that merge to form what I refer to as performance energy.

I believe that the key to performing at your best consistently over time is to build awareness of yourself and to create a keener sense of how the things around you impact your thoughts.

How does the experience of standing on the first tee with an audience of other golfers watching you impact your ability to access your skills? Does it make you feel nervous? And if it does, can you identify the thinking that produces that nervousness?

If you can identify the thinking, you are well on your way toward increased awareness. And then, you can do something about unproductive thoughts.

For example, you might realize you are nervous because you don't want to be embarrassed by duffing your tee-ball into the woods. You don't want the harsh judgment of others. Understandable.

But what's another way to look at that? Perhaps all the guys behind you want nothing better than to see you hit it well. They, too, can hit it into the woods, but in their minds, they are behind you, pulling for you to hit a great shot.

Or perhaps they don't care that much at all. So, then, you can forget about all that worry and anxiety. After all, it's just misplaced energy.

All that is left is for you to step up, hit it where you want to, and accept that you can handle the results, no matter where the ball goes.

We talked a lot last week about increasing

awareness of what is happening on the golf course to play better.

But here's the interesting thing: you can practice increasing your awareness all day, anywhere you go. In traffic, at work, and in your interactions with colleagues or those closest to you. Every day, there are opportunities to tune into the thought patterns driving how you interpret your experiences.

My message to the group last week is the same message I offer here. If you want to improve how you play on the golf course, practice growing your awareness of self whenever you can, and not only on the golf course, putting green, or during play.

Try it this week. You will be surprised at how easy it is.

Opportunities are everywhere.

Chapter 26
Mastery Orientation

This essay was inspired by the work of Bruce D Schneider—a brilliant mentor, coach, and psychotherapist (...as well as an accomplished amateur athlete and golfer) who developed an amazing system for coaches like me to help my clients perform better when it matters most. Bruce has helped me to understand the benefits of operating in any performance domain from a mindset rooted in the concept of elevating competence rather than trying to prove competence.

Your brain is amazing.

It regulates your body process, allows you to analyze and interpret external stimuli, and is the source of the very consciousness that allows you to read this sentence.

It is also an incredible survival tool.

The brain has a very powerful (but primitive) threat response system designed to keep you alive. Great when you need to run from a tiger (as you may have needed to 50,000 years ago), but not so great when you want to perform at your best in a competitive situation (like during the spring member-guest) against your buddies.

Your brain's threat response system monitors your external environment to determine whether your safety is in jeopardy, like a software program running silently in the background. You probably aren't even aware of it.

The challenge with this system is that it is not smart enough to know the difference between a saber-toothed tiger running toward you (which could actually harm you) and a slippery downhill ten-footer on the eighteenth hole to tie your match.

In both cases, your brain goes into threat response because it has assessed that you might lose something very important to you. It signals to your body that you are in danger.

The problem? On the golf course, this response has physical and mental implications. Sweaty palms impact your ability to hold the putter properly. Nervous, shaking hands affect your ability to move the putter as you want. And clouded judgment can influence the decision-making that keeps you in your process.

So, what to do?

I believe we can succeed more consistently in nearly any performance context when we do certain things to prevent the brain's threat response from activating.

I coach my clients on the distinction between

operating from a Mastery Orientation versus operating from an Outcome Orientation. And I teach them to adopt a Mastery Orientation whenever stepping into any performance arena.

The primary difference between the two operating orientations is this: people who operate from a Mastery Orientation are concerned with elevating their competence. People who operate from an Outcome Orientation are concerned with proving their competence.

Because of this, a golfer with a Mastery Orientation has a distinct performance advantage. They are more likely to stay connected to all their skills and abilities. And they can execute at a high level and do things like:

- tune into their surroundings in productive ways
- stick to their game plan and make clear decisions
- stay in the present moment and execute their process
- feel the putter move freely
- be playful and play the game.

This is because they are not wrapped up in results. To them, outcomes are important, but only insomuch as they reflect where the golfer is on their own path to mastery.

They know deep down that the worst that can happen is they will learn something about their game, their capacity for resilience, or their ability to compete in certain conditions. Because they hold this knowledge, their brain's primitive threat response is not activated as easily.

When they hit wayward shots, they see those shots in the context of their overall goals in golf—and not as defining moments in that particular competition, nor how they define their self-worth.

In a way, golfers who operate from a Mastery Orientation have written a story for themselves about what their experiences on the golf course mean to them. They access that story each time they play.

For them, golf is not (entirely) about winning or losing but rather about growing in their mastery of the game. No matter the stakes, each shot is an opportunity to learn and improve, not a challenge.

The result? They play better, score better, and typically enjoy themselves more.

On the other hand, the golfer who operates from an Outcome Orientation is typically in for a much more emotionally charged ride on the course. Why? Because their Ego is heavily involved in how they see each shot. They are trying to prove their competence rather than develop it.

When they stand at the first tee, they experience anxiety because they are trying to show the world the fruits of all their hard work on the range. We call this pressure.

When facing that slippery downhill ten-footer, the dominant thoughts are not about what they could gain but what they might lose. They experience what my colleague and NHL hockey performance coach Walter Aguilar likes to call horizontal thinking. They "move horizontally," out of the present moment and into the future, imagining how awful it would be to miss the putt and lose credibility with their friends or competitors.

As a result, they begin to lose access to their high-level cognitive functioning and the physical skills and abilities they had before starting the round. Of course, this can start a kind of performance death spiral that is difficult to pull out of.

The good news is that you have options. You can choose your mental and emotional stance when you play. You can choose the orientation you want to adopt when playing golf.

I hope you choose a Mastery Orientation.

Chapter 27
Miss It Fast

As the larger-than-life character that he was, Moe Norman was incredibly quotable. If you have seen any of Moe's videos, you know that he loved to be playful about the concepts he was trying to teach his audience. One of his go-to concepts is featured in the reflection below: Miss it Fast.

Moe never hovered over the ball before a shot. He knew that all the thinking about the shot was over at that point, and all that was left once he addressed the ball was to make a swing at it. He knew that most golfers missed most of their shots, so in a fun way, he was saying something like, "For heaven's sake, people, why not try something different? Why not just step up and hit the darn ball instead of spending an eternity trying to figure out what to do? After all, if you are going to miss it, why not get it over with."

Moe Norman said many memorable things throughout his life through his brilliance, the pursuit of excellence, and his perspective on life and golf.

One of my favorites is "Miss It Fast."

What does it mean? And how does it relate to your golf game?

The concept of "Miss it Fast" is amazingly simple yet rooted in the complex dynamics of the human brain. Even if Moe was unaware of it, the knowledge of what "Miss It Fast" yields for athletes like golfers is supported by the latest research and science in human performance and has surprising implications for your mental game.

Last weekend, at the 2-Day Mental Game Playing School at Prairie Landing Golf Club in West Chicago, a group of Single Plane Swing golfers had the opportunity to gain a much deeper understanding of what Moe meant by "Miss it Fast."

One of the key concepts we spent a lot of time on was this: The golf swing is a physical movement. A part of your brain called procedural memory is dedicated to replicating the physical movements you perform repeatedly.

When you rely on procedural memory to execute a golf shot, you give yourself the best chance of pulling off the shot as you intend to. However, when your brain's thinking and analytical parts are involved, you may struggle to create high-quality shots.

What to do?

Create routines or distractions to prevent too much thinking and analysis, which occur in the part of the brain associated with working memory. Hitting the ball relatively quickly is a perfect example of this kind of distraction.

One super-effective portion of the instruction last weekend was dedicated to teaching a tightly rehearsed, five-to-seven-second pre-shot routine based on the fundamental concept that dwelling over your shot for ten or fifteen seconds is a surefire way to take you out of procedural memory and into working memory where analysis, fear, and anxiety lurk.

Tim Graves and Chandler Rusk led the group through an exercise that allowed the guys at the school to see first-hand how much a short, crisp pre-shot routine can impact the mental game.

Elite-level golfers know this routine supports great shots but may not know why.

The reason is that when you keep your preshot routine short and structured, you prevent the over-analysis, anxiety, and resulting tightness in the swing from thinking too much about the shot you are about to hit.

When Todd or Tim Graves talk about "playing empty," they are referring to hitting shots when you operate from procedural memory versus working memory. They know, like Moe, that if you dwell and linger over shots before you hit them, your capacity to hit great shots is significantly diminished.

So, if you want to enhance your mental game, consider practicing your pre-shot routine. See if you can build a deliberate, but not rushed, routine that allows you to step into the ball and pull the trigger within five to seven seconds. You may not get "stuck" in your thinking nearly as often as you do now.

Miss it Fast!

Chapter 28
Stay Curious, My Friends

Curiosity is such an unsung mental game concept. Not many people talk about it. I like to think of curiosity as a mental bridge between the thoughts and feelings that limit our performance potential on the course and those that allow us to play our best golf. When I wrote this article, I had been working with a corporate client focused on cultivating curiosity because they knew it could help their leaders perform better under pressure. They were studying Larry Senn, the father of the modern corporate culture movement, and his strategies for moving from struggle and frustration to more productive feelings like optimism, wisdom, and creativity. Senn believes that curiosity can shut down negative thinking and allow higher-level thinking to dominate inside organizations and all performance domains—work, relationships, and on the golf course.

Last year, my wife and I joined a bowling league with many friends and now bowl once a month from September to May. It's been a lot of fun learning what it takes to be more consistent, roll the ball where I want to, and post higher scores.

Since I'm pretty competitive, I wanted to play at a high level if I could. So, I got my shoes and was fitted with a new ball, plus bag, rosin, slide powder, ball cleaner, the works!

For those of you who bowl, you already know that bowling is complicated, with many subtleties and nuances. It's pretty fascinating.

For as long as I can remember, bowling has been a family holiday tradition. And this year was no different, except that we bowled twice while our boys were home. During one of the games, my son Joe decided he wanted to try my ball, so he rolled it a few times.

My new bowling ball is a "hook ball" that will hook to the left for a right-hander like me. It requires a different delivery methodology than a "straight" ball. So, it has taken me a little while to get used to it.

Joe is a pretty levelheaded thinker. He immediately knew he must have done something incorrectly when he threw the ball. But he was calm and collected and, in essence, turned to me and said, "How did that look?"

I offered him some thoughts on how he could get closer to the model as I understood it, and he gave it another try. He got a lot closer this time, and the ball had a nice, gentle right-to-left hook. Not perfect. But he made progress right away.

I believe that Joe's success came from a willingness to be open to feedback and genuine curiosity about the process. He wasn't stuck in his story or impacted by imperfect results. He took action, observed, and tried to analyze what he saw. All without a lot of negative emotion, even though he didn't get the results he wanted.

When was the last time you were curious about something? You know that feeling of genuine interest in and wonder about what is happening, how something works, or how to improve a specific thing.

When we are truly curious, we are in a state where we are optimally receptive and open to discovery. Being curious can be fun.

The journey of improving in bowling, our golf swing—or anything—is always enhanced when we become curious, but expectation often shows up instead. When this happens, our emotional state intensifies as we measure reality against our story about what should happen. This is not a great plan for maintaining a productive performance mindset.

Frustration, anger, and irritation at the things that go "wrong" often shape how we experience challenges. But it doesn't have to be that way. You can shift your thinking and outcomes by anchoring to curiosity in difficult moments.

What does curiosity sound like?

When you hit the driver OB on your first hole, instead of, "Way to go, you big dummy," try "Hmmm. That's interesting. I wonder why that happened?"

When you miss that important putt, instead of, "You are the worst human being ever," try, "That's interesting. What can I learn from that?"

I know it seems a little far-fetched to engage in that kind of dialogue with yourself, but believe me, it works.

You have the right to be angry. But that anger may cause you to disconnect from your best thinking and, ultimately, your ability to perform well.

Larry Senn, the author of *Up the Mood Elevator*, says that leaders must be more curious if they want to perform at their best. He said that leaders who can be curious about the things happening in front of them are far more likely to tap into the best version of themselves.

Why? Because being curious creates a different feeling for us. It allows us to stay open, objective, and less judgmental or annoyed.

The same is true for anyone who wants to perform at their best. Anywhere. Anytime.

As you start the new year and think about what you want to accomplish on the golf course, think about a commitment to cultivating curiosity, creating a sense of wonder and real discernment that can lead to leaps in your skill and performance development.

So perhaps we can borrow a motto for 2018 by modifying one from a famous beer commercial.

Stay curious, my friends.

Chapter 29
Think Give, Not Get

Life and golf (same thing, right?) are so paradoxical. What looks like the right path to our desired outcome is often the path of struggle and difficulty. What seems like the wrong way to go is the exact line we should be taking. For example, bombing it down the fairway does not come from swinging harder but from achieving a kinematic sequence rooted in human mechanics and physics. Achieving lower scores is often not a function of making more birdies but fewer bogies or doubles.

One of the most profound mental game paradoxes I know of is rooted in the differences between getting and giving. It is rooted in the psychological comparison between grasping and clawing at something you desperately need (Hello, Ego!) versus having the presence of mind to focus on making a difference for the people around you. The essay below was meant to encourage the reader to consider what it would be like for them to operate from a GIVE instead of a GET mentality on the course.

I had lunch a couple days ago with an old buddy of mine from high school, Jon. We live about an hour from each other and don't see each other enough. You know how that goes.

I have noticed that the older we get, the more our conversations seem to be about the important aspects of our lives: family, clients, and experiences. Earlier in our careers,, we focused on acquiring—things, customers, new homes, new cars, new and better jobs, the right schools for our kids, etc.

Acquiring takes a ton of mental and emotional energy; that's probably why I remember feeling exhausted from the "chase." GIVING, in contrast, is different.

Jon commented that when he focuses on giving, his life becomes richer. The more he gives time to others, the more he gets back. The more he lets go of the idea of "getting" things from an interaction or a relationship, the easier, more fulfilling, and more abundant his life becomes.

You may have experienced this as well. I know I have in multiple areas of my life.

We know we are at our best when we stop trying to GET and make GIVING our primary mission. Our religious and spiritual traditions have cultivated a similar idea for thousands of years.

If you are struggling with golf, consider that you may be trying to get something from the game. Consider that the same paradigms of giving and getting apply to golf and that you may have been overly focused on yourself. (Your Ego may be trying to fill what it thinks is an unmet need.) Also, consider that you may be holding too tightly to a story about what you need in that round, on that course, in that tournament, etc.

If you learn to operate from a perspective rooted in the concept of giving, your golf experience could change significantly for the better. You would no longer feel the pull of the Ego. You would no longer feel the duality of winning and losing. You would see the game from a new perspective.

So, in this season of giving, stop trying to *get* something from the game of golf. Start thinking about what you can *give* the game, your playing partners, and your competition. When you get off yourself and focus on contributing, making a difference, and serving others, you set yourself up to play your best golf.

Chapter 30
A Little Inspiration

The essay below was about struggle. But there is a little more struggle that I did not write about. In September 2019, I broke my right (trail side) collarbone on a mountain bike trail. That meant that I played zero golf in the fall of 2019. The good news is that I recovered well, and by the time I wrote the essay below, my collar bone had healed, and my old AC impingement had reared itself on my left (lead-side) shoulder. I was such a baby about it. Six weeks after I wrote this article, I broke and displaced my left (lead-side) collarbone on the same mountain bike trail and had to have it surgically repaired. So, for a long stretch in 2019–2021, I had two fairly significant injuries to overcome. It wasn't always easy. That said, the darkness I felt about my whole situation was lessened greatly by the inspiration I took from Sophia Popov.

Sophia Popov didn't quit even when nobody would have blamed her if she had.

Because of her perseverance, she is now a major champion with full playing status on the LPGA Tour, having won the Women's Open last weekend at Royal Troon in Scotland.

Until recently, Popov could, at best, be described as an aspiring tour player. She had never gained more than conditional status on the LPGA Tour from 2015 to 2019. The reasons include the following:

- She missed securing her tour card by one stroke at the 2019 LPGA Tour Q School.
- Her only option in the spring of 2020 was to play Cactus Tour events in Arizona. She won three times in April and May but only collected $8,800 in winnings.
- She earned a spot in the 2020 Women's Open by placing ninth at the Marathon Classic in Toledo, OH in early August.
- She was ranked 304th in the world going into the Women's Open.

During the trophy presentation at Royal Troon, Popov said: "I almost quit playing last year. Thank God I didn't."

A big part of her struggle over the previous six years was her battle with Lyme disease, which went undiagnosed for a long time. Wow.

Her story speaks to me because of my challenges that season. It reminds me that there are likely many others on the Single Plane Swing journey who are also working through challenges and struggles.

In my case, an old shoulder injury reappeared for me. A lead-side shoulder AC impingement affects my ability to properly move into the impact position.

While I have been able to produce a swing that looks as close to the model as ever, when it comes to playing on the course and hitting a ball on the turf, my condition has led to some pretty sketchy ball striking.

I've posted some decent scores—the short game has been solid at times. (Have you tried the new Callaway Jaws wedges...I highly recommend them!) But the ball striking just has not been there—and honestly, it has been a challenge for me mentally, if not outright frustrating.

On my good days, even when I am not playing well, I enjoy being out there—practicing or playing. But on my bad days, I wonder why the heck I am doing this.

I've even thought about putting the clubs down for a while. You know...screw 2020. All of it. ... and look ahead to 2021.

Like you, I want to be able to hit the ball "pure." I want to know where the ball is going when I hit it. I want to know that it will fly the distance I envision. Is that too much to ask?

So, when Popov said, "I almost quit playing last year. Thank God I didn't," I got it. Her words inspired me to examine my thinking about where I was, where I am, and where I want to go.

I decided to revisit some truths.

The truth is that I am not striking the ball great right now.

It is also true that I have made significant strides in replicating the Single Plane Swing model. I can take this swing model progress and build on it, knowing that as I get in better physical shape to hit the ball, I will get where I want to be.

The truth is, I have made progress with my shoulder, and if I stay on my physio plan, I will be much more comfortable hitting shots again soon.

The truth is that I am not my golf game, even though sometimes I think I am.

Sophia Popov reminded me that this game feels like struggle sometimes. But struggle makes growth possible. Sometimes, when we break through struggle we achieve heights we could not have imagined.

So, now I am rededicated to the plan. Ready to embrace and enjoy the process of getting back to better ball striking. All of it.

If you are struggling, I encourage you to take Sophia Popov's story to heart. Perhaps it will inspire fresh thinking for you as it did for me.

Chapter 31
A Great Lesson

Sometimes, the greatest lessons in life and golf come when you least expect them. But you must be open to them. The essay below chronicles a classic inside-game lesson I learned in the spring of 2019. It's a story with many elements: Ego, self-worth, awareness, alertness, objectivity, truth, and a willingness to hear and accept what your coach tells you. The big takeaway for me (besides learning to club-up more often) was how powerful the Ego is when we play. The Ego can fog our decision-making and trap us into believing in an identity tied to how far we should hit a specific club. Unless we tune up our awareness, we hardly ever know it is happening.

Last week, I got one of the best lessons I've ever had on a golf course, but not for reasons you might imagine.

I stood on the tee at the seventeenth hole at Eagle Creek in Lake Nona, FL, with all the confidence I thought I needed. The shot was 188 yards over water to a large, undulating green bunkered in the front and the back.

My decision was easy. I would go with 6-iron. Why? Once, a couple of years earlier, I flushed a 6-iron pin-high to a hole 186 yards away. That became my 6-iron yardage forever. Isn't that how it works?

My playing companions that day were Chris Anderson, a terrific Single Plane Swing golfer from Detroit, MI, and GGA Master Instructors and superb ball-strikers Chandler Rusk and Trent White.

I watched Chandler and Trent hit one solid shot after another throughout our round. At the same time, I spent the first seven holes of our back nine, thinning one shot after the next. Chris wasn't having his best round but had also hit plenty of quality shots.

Importantly, as Trent would later observe, I had not reached a single green up to that point. In the words of Mike Tyson, I must have been in "bolivion."

At #17, we discussed the shots we were about to hit. I realized Trent and Chris planned to hit way more club than I planned. Trent looked at me half-incredulously as if to say, "You're kidding, right?"

"But, but, but....," I protested silently. "I hit that great 6-iron at Coffee Creek in Edmond, OK, in September 2016."

Sheepishly, I walked back to the cart and grabbed a 5-iron. Then I slapped at that one, hit it thin (again), and landed it about ten yards short.

Trent and Chandler, ever the gentlemen, chuckled a little and did a little #SMH. We laughed at the irony and finished the round.

Later, over dinner, Trent gently broke the news to me that I had played an exceptionally clueless round of golf. He wanted to know when I would learn to set the Ego aside and play more club. (Those are my words, not his.)

For a moment, his feedback hit me pretty hard. I'm the mental game coach, right? How could I be so unaware? Wasn't awareness my thing? Once I settled into Trent's feedback more objectively, I listened to him and heard what he said. I tuned into the objective truth rather than relying on my story.

I knew I had shorted myself repeatedly and never made the proper adjustments I could have made. The corrective action was simple—play with more awareness and, most importantly, club-up.

Sometimes, the Ego impairs our decision-making, and we are completely unaware of its interference. This impacts how we play the game. On that day, my Ego would not settle for attempting the shot on #17 with anything less than a 6-iron because my self-worth was on the line.

In fact, every time I stood over the ball, I was convinced I could pull off the shot I was hoping for, even though there was little evidence it would be possible on that day.

Trent and Chandler reminded me that I don't

have to be trapped in the idea that I'm "supposed to" hit a 6-iron 188 yards. That is not what makes me a better golfer, and it does not prove I'm a better human being.

They helped me see that our clubs are simply tools or implements. Golf is played well when you get good at choosing the best tool for the job in each moment. The number on the bottom of the club doesn't matter.

They taught me (again) that staying attuned to the results I produce on the course (what I call "objective reality") will help me make better decisions on the course.

It was not my best round of golf, but the experience held an amazing lesson for me, thanks to Trent and Chandler.

So, get out there and have fun. But for heaven's sake, stay alert and club-up!

Chapter 32
Practice Slower & Play Faster

Sometimes, we do things in exactly the opposite way we should. We typically practice on the range too quickly because we are not maintaining command over our mental game. On the course—because we feel the consequences of making mistakes more acutely—we slow everything down as if that will help. In the essay below, I reference two terrific resources—The Talent Code by Daniel Coyle and Choke by Sian Beilock—to help you overcome two of the biggest challenges for amateur golfers.

That sounds like a directive. Right?

Actually, I think of it as a mental game approach. Why? At almost every Graves Golf school I attend, many students are doing their level best to achieve the Single Plane Swing model. However, many, if not most, suffer because of two important missteps.

They practice too quickly, and they play too slowly.

Interestingly, these are not execution missteps caused by a lack of focus or an inability to understand a strategy—they are mental game failures.

Let me explain, starting with the concept of practicing slower.

The Single Plane Swing curriculum that Todd and Tim Graves and their instruction team refined over the years is based on the latest skill development research: we learn best from slow, deliberate, and proper practice movements, not by beating balls over and over again.

One cannot groove and assimilate new body positions without this slow work.

Moe Norman famously told Todd and Tim that he once held his finish position for an entire day. Why? Moe said he wanted to "make it stronger."

Just last week, I heard Todd tell the story about when one of their Master Instructors was converting from conventional to the Single Plane Swing; he spent hours on the practice range working on one thing: perfecting his move into position one.

Why won't most students spend their practice time like this? One word—Ego.

It's more satisfying for the Ego to hit one great shot every once in a while than to spend the time needed to master a position or two.

In other words, even though it is a rational enough concept—practicing slowly during your swing development—it is hard because part of your brain wants to show the world what you are capable of.

The harsh reality is that you will delay the mastery of the Single Plane Swing until you slow down and develop a deliberate practice regimen that includes far more correct body movement and fewer shots with a ball. That's just the way it is.

Slowing down requires cultivating awareness of your Ego trying to sabotage such a regimen. You need to practice tuning into your mental and emotional tendencies and discipline yourself to stay on track with the deliberate, deep practice that will yield the changes you want.

Dan Coyle wrote about this in *The Talent Code*. Todd and Tim often refer to Coyle's research and insights. Skill development comes from deep, deliberate, proper practice.

Now, let's address when to play faster. When it comes to golf, most players play too slowly. Specifically, they tinker and hover too long over the ball before hitting their shots. This causes paralysis by analysis.

Sian Beilock, in *Choke*, chronicles the trouble we get into when we linger over a golf shot too long. She explains that the part of our brain responsible for moving the body in space—procedural memory—switches off in those moments, and our working memory takes over. The shift causes overthinking and less-than-optimal muscle movement, which often causes the choke.

The antidote? Play faster. Stop lingering. Pull the trigger on your shots sooner. This will prevent overthinking and allow you to play golf more as a reactionary sport and execute shots that align with your talent level.

So, if you want to improve this year, do yourself a favor and tune up your mental game skills. Discipline yourself to practice slower when off the course and play faster when on it.

Have Fun!

Chapter 33
My Lesson in Acceptance

The reflection below is about what may have been one of the most important turning points in my golf development. As I think about the story in this article from the spring of 2019, I am imagining what Yoda would have said to me when I was challenged by one of the best instructors in the game. It might have been something like: "Strong in you the defensiveness is, young Jedi." That's because I had assumed a defensive posture, and my Ego was protecting my precious little identity at a moment that called for listening, hearing and accepting. I eventually got there, but not without a little struggle. It was a great lesson about being a better student and staying on a path of growth and development instead of comfort and certainty.

How good a student are you? How willing are you to accept feedback from your coach? Consider cultivating acceptance as a key mental component of your Single Plane Swing journey.

I was on the Graves Golf Academy range with Tim Graves and GGA master instructor James Bell recently at Eagle Creek Golf Club in Florida. We were in the middle of a 5-Day Alumni Camp, chatting through a short lull in the action as we waited for a group of students to return to the range from the clubhouse.

Tim and James started playing a few games on the range. Tim shouted, "Highest shot!" He and James went head-to-head, attempting to hit the highest shots with their 7 irons. I was down the range, working on my swing but within earshot. The banter between them was fun, but the competition was real—each wanted to "win."

Soon after, Tim announced, "Lowest shot!" It was breezy, with winds steady at 15–20 mph. Tim and James are Oklahoma golfers who know how to hit it low. But Tim Graves's "stinger" is something special. Advantage Tim.

I got excited because I've always wanted to learn that shot. So, from down the range, I shouted, "I'm in on this one, guys!" and started hitting shots. The first shot I hit was awesome—at least, I thought it was! The ball felt so pure on the club head and took off straight into the wind. Then it went up, up and up. Not exactly a low stinger.

So I hit another one. Again, it was pure and dead straight. To me, it was a great-looking ball, but like the first ball, it was way too high.

Then it happened—a candid and abrupt challenge that shook me up a bit. Ultimately, the challenge taught me an amazing lesson about acceptance and how to be a better student when being coached.

The challenge came from Tim at the end of the range. "Terrible shot!"

Huh? How could that be a terrible shot? I had hit it so pure and straight. *Why was he leaning in so hard?*

Tim shot back again. "Brutal! You're dead with that shot!"

Wow. That was a little harsh.

My sensitive Ego wants people to like me, and I struggled to make sense of his approach. I tried to laugh it off. "Hey! Quit being so mean to me!"

Then Tim did something brilliant.

He replied, "Oh, so you want me to treat you like a child? Go easy on you? Tell you that you are hitting the ball just fine? That you are doing great? Fine. But if you want to really learn how to be a player, you are going to have to figure out shots like this. And right now, you aren't even close."

Whoa!

In retrospect, I think he meant, "You are not listening, Paul. You are not accepting my feedback. You are not hearing that the shot you hit will not work in these conditions. You are too wrapped up in your own Ego. You need to learn to hit a different shot."

He was right. My Ego had gone into action, trying to defend my honor and credibility. Part of me wanted to run home to my mommy—for real.

But then something inside me woke up, and I realized this might be an amazing learning opportunity. I realized I needed to accept what Tim said as the truth and deal with that instead of trying to satisfy my Ego or emotional sensitivities.

I decided to stop defending my inability to create the shot I was attempting and surrender to the moment. I remember thinking that as uncomfortable as I was that second, I was about to grow as a golfer and maybe even as a person.

I think Tim sensed I was uncomfortable but also that I was game for learning something—another sign of a great coach.

Tim challenged me athletically and mentally in ways I had not been challenged before. He told me what to do but left it up to me to figure it out. I think he believed I could get there, but not without more focus and intentionality about what I was trying to achieve—hit it low, powerful and boring, and with compression.

I began listening to what he was saying objectively and without judgment.

"Lower. Do it again. Lower. Come on. Get down and into the ball. Watch my hands. Do this."

Soon, I was getting closer and closer to producing the low "stinger" shot Tim was teaching me. My shots were no longer ballooning up into the wind. Although they weren't as low as I wanted, they behaved more like Tim's shots—low, boring, and straight.

I had finally figured out what it feels like to move

down and into the ball with a very "hands-forward" shaft lean, which allowed me to see a much different ball flight. I wasn't producing a shot that looked exactly like Tim's, but mine was closer than it had been.

How had I accomplished that?

I accepted my reality, stopped pushing back on my coach, and asked questions like, "How does that look?" and "Better?"

When we bring acceptance to our experiences, we see our reality more objectively and without judgment or personal sensitivity. That day, I dropped my need to defend myself to be a better listener and learner.

Tim taught me a great lesson that day about hitting a 7-iron as low as possible and accepting feedback from those trying to help me. He instinctively leaned on me a little at that moment, and I am very grateful he did.

As a coach, I want to be as candid as possible with my clients, as brutal as it may seem for them in the moment. As a student of the GGA swing model, I want to LOVE the idea of feedback instead of dreading or fearing it. Embracing feedback makes me better.

Acceptance is a powerful paradigm as you prepare to work on your golf game more regularly and get feedback from the GGA team in videos or in person at our live instruction schools. It will help you become a better student and, ultimately, a better player.

Chapter 34

It's Not Magic, or Is It?

Close-up magic is one of the most amazing entertainment experiences. I mean, how the heck do they do that, right? I met and interviewed a talented close-up magician, John Michael Hinton, a few years ago. His take on how he grows and develops as a magician and entertainer—his success formula—is a great lesson for anyone trying to perform at a higher level in any domain. I appreciate how he starts with one nonnegotiable element—hone your skills the best you can. His formula includes a couple more important elements—the willingness to put yourself "out there" and a focus on serving others, which means getting off yourself and your needs. We can apply Hinton's formula to golf.

According to his branding, John Michael Hinton is an amazing magician, speaker, and redhead. He is all those things and more, and no matter what you call him, he is an incredibly entertaining stage performer.

My wife Paula and I saw John perform in Cleveland in October, and we were blown away by what we saw. His specialty is close-up sleight-of-hand magic. He made cards and money disappear and reappear. He solved a Rubik's Cube without even touching it, and he blew my mind with a bag of Skittles.

I recently spoke with my new friend John about the performance dynamics of a stage performer like himself. I was curious about how the performance dynamics we see in leaders of organizations or athletes on the field of play, including golfers, show up for an elite-level magician/performer. He was kind enough to give me some time during his busy schedule on the road ahead of a show in Denver, CO.

It may surprise you, but there are many similarities between what we encounter on our Single Plane Swing journey and what John encounters on his performance journey. John told me that certain things he does as part of his success formula help to ensure he is in the proper mental state to perform his act. Some things can throw John off his game a bit, if only temporarily.

One thing he said reminded me of something I have discussed in this space and that you have heard many times from Todd, Tim, and the instruction team at Graves. John said most of his stage confidence results from the hours and hours he spends honing his skills. A well-known old quote captures his approach to developing as a performer—"Don't practice until you get it right.

Practice until you can't get it wrong."

He has modified the quote to align with the context in which he performs—"Don't practice until you get it right. Practice until you know all the ways it can go wrong." The bottom line is that, for John, there is no substitute for mastering the skill. The right kind of practice produces the performance energy he needs to be at his best.

John said he intentionally practices more than he thinks he needs to because putting in the hours gives him confidence.

John also shared that one of the secrets to his development as a performer is his willingness to take new tricks and illusions onto the road. He understands that part of his journey to mastery is putting his new performances to the test with live audiences. He knows he must "Road Test" parts of his act, which requires a willingness to be vulnerable. Taking a new performance on the road means he knows he may not have mastered the trick yet, but he's willing to subject himself to the negative judgment of others as part of his development process.

Finally, one of my most important insights came when John talked about his intention for every performance. When asked about his focus before each performance, he said he focuses on ensuring that people who experience his show *feel loved and cared for*.

That's right. It's not "I hope they all buy my T-shirts," or "I hope that the scout from America's

Got Talent likes my show," or "How much money am I gonna make from these people?" or "I hope they like me."

John's focus is on others. He knows that if he focuses on his purpose, which is to ensure that others feel loved and cared for, there is a much better chance he can perform at his best.

What does this have to do with golf? Suppose you approached each practice and game the way John Michael Hinton thinks about his performance on the stage?

- Practice more than you think you need to.
- Work on building your skills and your feel. There is no substitute for great mechanics and ball-striking skills for all elements of the game. It's the key to elevating your confidence on the first tee.
- Subject yourself often and willingly to the judgment of others. It will build your resilience and help you learn to play in front of others.
- Loosen your grip on your story about what it means to make a mistake in front of others. Mistakes are information. Embrace them. Mistakes help us learn and develop. Everyone makes them.
- Consider approaching the game, the course, and your playing partners with more love, gratitude, and appreciation. Make your golf experience about something other than ful-

filling your needs. Life is too short for that.

It works for John Michael Hinton. It can work for you, too.

It's not magic, but it might produce magical results for you.

Chapter 35
Critical Moments

Sometimes, what you do next profoundly impacts your performance on and off the golf course. In any round of golf, there are typically inflection points. I call them critical moments. If we handle them appropriately, such moments can help us become better players. In the essay below, I recall a seemingly innocuous moment during a round of golf that stuck with me as a great example of how to move successfully through a setback. We have choices to make each time we play about how to move past the inevitable mishits or lousy bounces. We can wallow in the setbacks and challenges. Wallowing is not always a choice or conscious decision but rather a reflexive threat response. Instead of wallowing, we can learn something from critical moments.

Last week, I played with Single Plane Academy student Chris Anderson at his course in Detroit. Chris is a very good player and has worked a lot on his swing mechanics over the years. Chris has also focused on his mental game skills for the past year, and I'm proud of what he has accomplished in that arena.

What Chris did after a mid-round disappointment was a great lesson for me on handling critical moments we face when we play.

The fifth hole is a 355-yard, significant dogleg right par four. It's a bit of a placement hole off the tee. Chris hit a perfect drive (4-wood, I think) to put himself into position to shoot at the green. (If you want to see what a very strong tee-ball game looks like, go play with Chris.)

On his second shot, Chris slightly missed a 5-hybrid and left his ball in the deep rough, short and right of the green. With the pin back and left, Chris had a good angle to the hole and could still get up and down for par.

He stepped up and hit a chip a bit firm, running it through the green and coming to rest on the back fringe but against the rough about twenty-five feet from the hole. Ouch. Now, it was another difficult chip for par.

His next shot made its way down toward the hole to about ten feet, and he missed the bogey putt. Double bogey. Four shots to get down from the greenside rough. That one stung!

What Chris did next really impressed me. Shooting 6 on that hole was frustrating, but he did not dwell on the score. Instead, he went right to, "What can I learn from this?" Chris understands that there is opportunity in our mistakes. He knows that scoring a 6 on a 350-yard par four does not make him less of a person.

After we finished the hole, I heard him mention how he could have approached that differently. He said, "Well, I guess the lesson here is to first be on the green and not to get too cute with these kinds of shots when the pin is there."

Then he dropped a ball in the rough from where he hit his third shot, popped a little chip to the center of the green, and watched as it collected to about eight feet from the hole. I could see that Chris had made an important yet calm and measured mental note about that experience.

There are what I call critical moments that we all face when we play. I call them critical because what happens next is *critical* to staying in a productive performance mindset.

Chris had a choice about how to think about what he experienced on hole #5 and what he would think, say, and do about it. In that critical moment, Chris chose to connect to the lesson that was there for him rather than devolving into struggle or frustration because he had played the hole badly.

As a result, Chris:

- Became more aware of his mental and emotional dynamics—Moe called that Alertness.
- Loosened his grip on his story about what should be happening—Moe called that Indifference.
- Captured the true lesson of the moment that

helped him on his journey to mastery.

You can do the same thing when you play. It takes awareness that a critical moment has occurred. It also requires intentionally anchoring productive thinking in the moment to deal with the critical moment when it shows up on the course.

What will you do next time you face a critical moment on the course?

Chapter 36
It's the Journey

Golf is one of the most incredible games. It teaches us so much if we let it. The most productive way to see this game is as a journey toward growth and enlightenment. Yes, the goals and outcomes matter. But it's just as important to find ways to enjoy every bit of both the journey and the adventure. The good. The struggle. The great shots. The not-so-great ones. Ultimately, our capacity to bring context and perspective to what matters most to us determines whether we can show up at our best, perform to our potential, and enjoy this game as much as possible.

In early 2015, I realized I had visited nearly all fifty states in America except Idaho and Montana. It occurred to me that I would be turning fifty that year. If I got a little intentional, I could complete the "50 States x 50 Race" (I think I made up) by visiting all the states before I turned fifty. What an incredible accomplishment that would be! Right?

I worked through the logistics: I would fly to Spokane, WA, then drive to Coeur d'Alene, ID.

While there, I could play some golf and then make my way over to Montana, which is only a short distance from Coeur d'Alene. My buddy Jon from high school, who is always up for an adventure, would come with me. The trip was on.

Jon and I hopped on a flight in May of that year and headed out on our adventure. On day one, we traveled to Idaho—#49–check! On day two, we played golf at the Coeur d'Alene Resort, famous for its movable island green. (I got the certificate.) On day three, we drove an hour or so east to the Montana border—#50–check! The race was over. I won!

Cue the big celebration, right? The elation. The pure joy. The confetti.

I experienced none of those things. Frankly, it was a bit of a letdown and even a bit ironic.

I said to myself, "You did what? Traveled all this way just to be able to tell your friends you traveled to fifty states?"

This essay is starting to feel like a giant humble brag.

But the truth is that I had an amazing three days with a lifelong buddy who enjoys many of the things I do. Golf, adventure, great conversations about the meaning of life, etc. That was where the joy and happiness were for me. If I reflect on my journey through the other forty-eight states, I can also think of tons of great memories and experiences.

So, by the time I got to the Montana border, the "prize" didn't matter as much.

The point is that it's not about the destination but the journey. Always has been. Always will be.

When I was younger, I thought that was just another platitude. Pure garbage. A phrase invented by people who were too afraid or too timid to do what it took to get themselves across the finish line.

I don't believe that anymore. I am most energized when working toward something and engaged purposefully in pursuing a goal, dream, or defined outcome. On the path. On the journey.

I am immensely satisfied when I reach my goals and sometimes even elated. (Ask me about my experiences walking across the Grand Canyon's Rim-to-Rim route the next time you see me.) Looking back, it really was the journey that mattered most. Looking ahead, I believe it really is the journey that matters most.

The journey is what points you. It energizes, challenges, and puts you into a productive struggle that creates growth. (Thank you, Dan Coyle.)

Learning to play golf at a higher level the way you are doing it is a journey. Remember to enjoy it. Relish it. Know what it is and isn't. It is an amazing adventure of learning and growth. It is not your identity. It is not an obstacle to overcome but an experience to move through that will change you forever.

Dr. Jordan Peterson writes in *Beyond Order*, "You

are not only something that is. You are something that is becoming."

Humans are teleological; we must have purpose. We must have targets. We must aim at a destination and travel in that direction. It is how we are wired. What truly brings joy, satisfaction, and happiness to life is not necessarily arriving at some pre-ordained goal but rather what we experience along the journey.

The next time you are struggling or feeling frustrated about your game or that shot that went sideways, stop. Take a deep breath and remind yourself, "It's about the journey." Consider the gift inherent in that moment and how the moment will make you stronger, smarter, and more able to complete the journey you are on. Remember that you are becoming—one little step at a time.

Safe Travels!

www.ingramcontent.com/pod-product-compliance
Lightning Source LLC
Chambersburg PA
CBHW051614010526
44107CB00037B/1429/J